The Bible Food Truck walks k ... food-centered way! Not only are they hearing Bible lessons chronologically, but kids are given a chance to apply God's truths to their lives with the "Faith To-Go" application at the end of each devotion. Kids will be challenged to think about God's Word, live out His teaching, serve His people, and make their own food truck. This devotion will be a family favorite, for sure. I can't wait to use it with my kids!

—**Amber Pike**, Children's Minister, KidzMatter Magazine
Editor & Author of *Exploring the Bible Through History*
and *The Family Cookbook Devotional*

Vanessa Myers always finds ways to help kids connect with God's Word, and *The Bible Food Truck* does exactly that! I love this food-truck-themed devotion for kids that invites them to dig into the Bible. Each devotion is straightforward and simple enough for kids to digest, but also deep enough to give them something to chew on and apply. The action steps at the end of each devotional help kids take their faith to go, and the overarching project of creating your own food truck is such a fun way to tie all of the devotions together. *The Bible Food Truck* is a fun and creative way to encourage kids to feast on God's Word!

—**Brittany Nelson**, Founder & Creator, Deeper KidMin

With busy, on-the-go lives, I've often been afraid my children's faith would become a sideliner in the hustle and bustle of the everyday. This devotional not only offers short, biblical reminders of God's faith and love, but it also gives practical steps where our children can take their faith "on-the-go." I love how Vanessa made the "food" of the Bible so accessible and easy to understand. My kids love these devotions!

—**Kristin Funston**, Christian women's speaker, Bible teacher, and author of *More for Mom: Living Your Whole & Holy Life*

A vocational devotional for kids! *The Bible Food Truck* is conversational with short sentences and kid-friendly vocabulary. Vanessa's children's ministry skills really shine through. She starts in Genesis and takes us through the Bible. Each of the 75 devotions begins with a scripture, a short conversational devotion with prayer, and ends with a next step she calls, "Faith To-Go." This interactive devotional is easily read aloud and would be perfect at meals wherever your table might be. Kids will use their imagination to build and plan their own food truck business as she takes them step-by-step through the process. This book would make a great gift from parents and grandparents and spark some great conversations about Jesus and business.

—**Dede Reilly**, Children's Ministry Consultant for the North Georgia Conference of the United Methodist Church, Children's Director at McEachern Memorial UMC, & Children's Ministry Blogger at: https://dede-bull-reilly.com/

I'm very thankful for the care and attention Vanessa pays to connecting the Scripture to the lives of our young ones. As both a pastor and a father, I'm always looking for everyday ways to make the Bible extra special for my family. To be able to see Jesus in the ordinary is such a necessary and special gift!

—**Rev. Whit R. Martin**, Pastor, Villa Rica First United Methodist Church

The "Faith To-Go" section really helped me understand how to practice the lessons, so that I can turn them into actions.

—**Laney Martin**, age 9

The scripture preview verses helped me better understand the Bible and how God works in different ways every day.

—**Maggie Martin**, age 8

THE BIBLE FOOD TRUCK

Serving Up 75 Devotions for Kids
About Food in the Bible

Vanessa Myers

For my daughters, Rae Lynn and Shelby.
May you always put God first in your life,
remember He is with you, and know He loves
you no matter what.

TABLE OF CONTENTS

ACKNOWLEDGMENTS

God is so good, right? I am so thankful to God for the ideas He gives me to help teach children about Him. I am always amazed at how much I learn about Him just from writing these devotions. Thank You, Lord, for the gift You have given me in teaching and writing about You.

Many thanks to my husband, Andrew, for always supporting me through my writing. Whenever I have a new idea for a book or a resource to write for families, he encourages me along the way. I love you, Andrew!

I am thankful for my sister, Luanne, whom I can bounce ideas off of and pick her creative brain for help with my book projects. Thanks for being the best big sister ever!

I am grateful for those who helped me along the way with all that needed to be done to get this book into your hands: Jessica Fralin for your amazing skills with editing, my good friend, Shana Corbin, for the awesome cover design and graphics, and Jen Stults for the wonderful formatting of this book. You ladies have helped me tremendously!

To God be the glory for the ways He will use this book to glorify His name!

INTRODUCTION

God is great, God is good. Let us thank Him for our food. By His hands, we are fed. Give us, Lord, our daily bread. Amen.

How many times have you said that blessing before a meal? Maybe too many to count. God gives us food to eat, and we thank Him for it. Prayers like this are our way of giving thanks to God for giving us food to eat.

Every day, God provides the food we need to eat in order to live. But that's not something new. God has been providing food for all creation since the beginning of time. How do we know that? Because we read about it in the Bible!

Have you ever thought about how many times food is mentioned in the Bible? This devotional will take you through lots of them! We'll study 75 Bible verses that mention food or drink (or fasting from them).

Are you a little surprised there are so many mentions of food and drink in the Bible? Me too! When I began writing this devotional, I had no idea I would find 75 different Bible stories that mention food. But there are even more than 75 mentions of food and drink in the Bible! One website says there are 1,207 mentions of food in the Bible.[1] While reading these Bible verses, I found myself learning new things about Bible stories I thought I knew already. Isn't it amazing that God helps us learn new things every time we read the Bible?

For every devotion, you will find Bible verses listed at the top for you to read (and I really hope you will open your Bible and read them). After you read the Bible story, take a few minutes to read the written devotion and pray the prayer I've shared with you. At the end of each devotion, you will find an action step, which I call "Faith To-Go." This section gives you one simple thing you can do that day to serve God, share His love, and grow your faith in Him. It

---

1 https://heraldcourier.com/lifestyles/devouring-the-bible-reveals-a-feast-of-references-to-food/article_53b35689-78cd-538c-bdc4-7d497abfacc7.html

also gives you a way to take your faith out into the world and share it with someone else.

So, why the food truck theme?

If you've ever been to a fair, a festival, or even a big party in your city, you may have seen a lot of food trucks. These trucks serve different types of food items. You might find one truck that serves barbecue, one that serves pizza, one that serves tacos, and another that serves ice cream. Many choices, but all of them will satisfy your hunger and taste delicious, too!

In some ways, I see the Bible like a food truck. It contains so many different kinds of stories. We have Old Testament stories about Moses, Joshua, David, and the prophets, as well as beautiful Psalms written as prayers and praises to God. We also have New Testament stories about Jesus, His disciples, the Church, Paul, and even what heaven will be like. There are 66 books of the Bible, and they all teach us so much about God, Jesus, and the Holy Spirit.

We read the Bible because we are hungry. I'm not talking about physical hunger, but spiritual hunger (which means we want to know more and more about God). No matter what book you choose, when you read the Bible, your hunger for God is satisfied, your thirst to know more about God is quenched, and you have peace and comfort knowing our God is great!

Here's a really fun part of this book...

You will get to create your own food truck! And not just any food truck. This will be a food truck you will use to serve God. Think about this: if you could serve God by having a food truck ministry, what type of food truck would you have? Wouldn't it be fun to drive around, serving your favorite food to people, and—the best part—telling them about Jesus?

Throughout this book, you'll find pages that will help you design your food truck. You will be able to do the following:

- Create a menu (figure out first what type of food you want to serve).
- Come up with a name and design a logo.
- Find a Bible verse to base your food truck on.

- Write out a mission statement (which is basically the reason why you are doing this).
- List out what kind of equipment you will need on your truck in order to cook the food.
- Write out a recipe for one menu item.
- Come up with a grocery list of all food supplies and other supplies you will need to stock your food truck.
- List out the type of employees (or workers) you want to help you.
- Share where your first stop will be.
- Write out a prayer to God to bless your food truck.
- At the very end of this book, you will get a chance to draw a picture of how your food truck will look when it is out on the road serving the Lord!

I pray you'll have lots of fun with this food truck and get creative with your designs, but most importantly, I pray you will learn more about God and draw closer to Him as you read about how God blesses us through food.

Buckle up! Let's go on a food truck adventure with God!

GOD CREATED FOOD

GENESIS 1:11-13, 29-30

Have you ever wondered where exactly food came from? How did we get fruits and vegetables to eat? How did we get meat to eat? How did we get food on the earth?

Well, cool story: God created it! In Genesis 1, we see the whole creation story laid out for us. God created everything on this earth. On the third day, God said, "Let the land produce vegetation: seed-bearing plants and trees on the land that bear fruit with seed in it, according to their various kinds" (Genesis 1:11).

God created the land, and He created the plants and trees that grow the food we need to eat. Think about all the food you eat. Where does it come from? The potatoes you eat are grown in the ground and God created them! The apples you eat are grown on a tree and God created them! The grapes you eat are grown on a vine and God created them! Our food is created by God, and He provides for us daily.

> ## GOD'S DAILY SPECIAL
>
> "Then God said, 'I give you every seed-bearing plant on the face of the whole earth and every tree that has fruit with seed in it. They will be yours for food.'"
> Genesis 1:29

Then, God told Adam and Eve that all of the seed-bearing plants He created would be their food to eat. They didn't have to wonder what they would eat, or if they would be hungry. They didn't have to figure out what God would provide them to eat. God told them exactly what their food would be.

Isn't that amazing? God created food to nourish us. He created every food on this earth to keep us full and satisfied. He gave us the food we would need to live on this earth.

So, next time you eat, thank God for every piece of food on your plate. Name them out loud: "Thank You, God, for mashed potatoes. Thank You, God, for macaroni and cheese. Thank You, God, for apple pie. Thank You, God, for chicken fingers. Thank You, God, for spinach. Thank You, God, for bread." I love to be specific when giving thanks because it reminds me that God deserves our praise for every specific thing on this earth. Thank You, God, for our food!

Creator God, thank You for creating food for me to eat. Help me to always remember You created food for me and help me to make healthy choices when I eat. In Jesus' name, Amen.

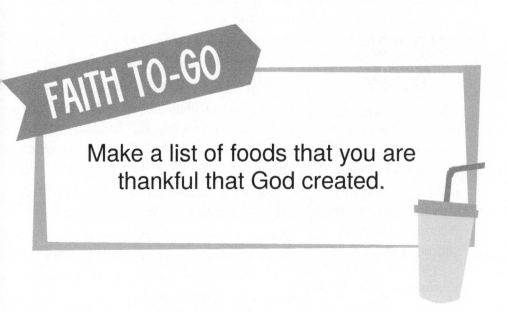

FAITH TO-GO

Make a list of foods that you are thankful that God created.

THE FORBIDDEN FRUIT

GENESIS 3

Want to try an experiment? You'll need a plate of chocolate chip cookies (it's best if they're fresh out of the oven—warm, gooey, and delicious), and you'll also need your parents.

Your parents will tell you that you can't eat any of the cookies while they are in the other room. Take a seat at your kitchen table and place the cookies right in front of you. Your parents will then leave you alone with the plate of cookies. Your job: see if you can resist the temptation to eat the cookies. Your parents told you not to, but don't they look delicious? Don't you want to try one? Can you resist the temptation to eat the cookies when your parents told you specifically not to? Go ahead and try this experiment and see what happens!

> ### GOD'S DAILY SPECIAL
>
> "When the woman saw that the fruit of the tree was good for food and pleasing to the eye, and also desirable for gaining wisdom, she took some and ate it."
> Genesis 3:6

Adam and Eve were faced with this same exact temptation. God gave them lots of food to eat. But He also gave them one rule: don't eat from the tree in the middle of the garden. Seems like an easy rule to follow, right?

But Adam and Eve had a hard time following this rule, all because of the serpent from today's story. The serpent made Eve rethink what God had actually told her. He tricked her into changing her mind and taking a bite of the fruit that was forbidden by God.

What happened when Eve took a bite? She loved it! In fact, she loved it so much that she had to share it with Adam. But after they both had eaten the forbidden fruit, their eyes were opened. They immediately realized they didn't have any clothes on and made some out of fig leaves.

Have you ever done the opposite of what your parents instructed? After you disobeyed, did you feel bad? Adam and Eve had done the opposite of what God had told them and they felt really bad.

Right after their eyes were opened and they knew things they hadn't known before, they heard God walking in the garden. They were so embarrassed and upset about what they did that they hid from God. They didn't want Him to find them because they were ashamed of what they had done.

But here's something I want you to remember: no matter what you do, even if it's something you know you should not do, God still loves you. There is nothing you can do that will make God stop loving you. He loves you no matter what. Just go to Him and seek forgiveness. He will forgive you, just like He forgave Adam and Eve... because He loved them. And He loves you, too.

Holy God, forgive me for the times I mess up and do the wrong thing. Help me to follow You every day. In Jesus' name, Amen.

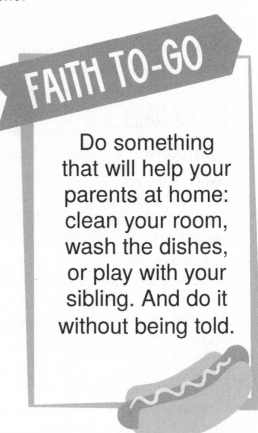

FAITH TO-GO

Do something that will help your parents at home: clean your room, wash the dishes, or play with your sibling. And do it without being told.

THE OLIVE LEAF

GENESIS 8:6-12

Noah had probably never been happier than he was in the moment he saw the dove flying back to the ark with an olive leaf in its mouth.

Yes, that's right. An olive leaf brought Noah and his family happiness.

Many of you probably know the story of Noah and the ark. God told Noah to build an ark and fill it with his family, along with two of every kind of animal and bird. God was going to bring a flood to destroy the earth and rebuild it, but He was going to save Noah and his family from that flood because of Noah's faithfulness to Him.

It rained and poured for forty days and nights. Can you imagine being on a boat for so many rainy days?! I would have been seasick every day. I think I would have been sad and lonely, too. That's a really long time to be stuck on a boat without anywhere else to go!

Finally, the rain stopped. To see if the land was dry enough for Noah and his family to get off the boat, he sent out a raven, and then a dove (three times). The second time the dove went out, it came back with an olive leaf in its mouth! That may not seem very exciting to you and me, but it was to Noah. The leaf was proof that the water had finally gone down enough for them to get off the boat! An olive leaf

GOD'S DAILY SPECIAL

"When the dove returned to him in the evening, there in its beak was a freshly plucked olive leaf! Then Noah knew that the water had receded from the earth."
Genesis 8:11

is found on an olive tree, which produces olives, of course! This little leaf was a sign of food on the earth!

Do you want to know how I can tell this olive leaf was an exciting thing for Noah? Go back to your Bible. Read Genesis 8:11. What punctuation mark comes after the words "olive leaf?" An exclamation point! So we can tell from this passage that the olive leaf was an exciting thing for Noah and his family.

I am sure Noah and his family had to be tired of whatever they were eating (the Bible doesn't tell us exactly what they ate while they were on the ark). I bet they were ready for something new to eat. They were ready to get off that boat and live a normal life again.

Sometimes, the small things in life (like the olive leaf for Noah) can bring us pure happiness. What simple things in life fill you with joy? If you don't know, look for them. What makes you smile? What do you love? When we can find joy in the simple things, we will find that our lives are peaceful and happy.

Heavenly Father, thank You for the joy of the simple olive leaf. Help me to remember that You are my joy and my salvation. In Jesus' name, Amen.

FAITH TO-GO

Do something for someone today that brings them joy.

ABRAHAM FEEDS THREE VISITORS

GENESIS 18:1-15

When guests come over to your house, do you feed them? I imagine that most of you do. Your parents probably make a trip to the grocery store to buy food to serve to your guests. You want to make sure they're well-fed while they are visiting your house!

That's exactly what Abraham did when three visitors came to his house one day. In Genesis 18, we find the story of the Lord appearing to Abraham near his home. The Lord appeared as three men, and while that might seem weird to us, Abraham knew immediately that this was a visit from God.

Abraham offered water to wash their feet and to rest under a tree, and he also offered to give them something to eat.

Abraham ran back to his tent and found his wife, Sarah, and they got busy cooking a meal for their three visitors. Sarah made some bread. Abraham went to pick out his best calf and had his servant prepare it. He also served some curds and milk. What a nice feast for his special guests!

> ### GOD'S DAILY SPECIAL
>
> "Let me get you something to eat, so you can be refreshed and then go on your way – now that you have come to your servant."
> Genesis 18:5

It was during this visit that Abraham found out that God was going to give them a son. The men told him they would return at the same time next year, and by then, Sarah would have a baby.

Guess what Sarah did when she heard this? She laughed! She thought that was funny because she was almost 90-years old. She thought she was too old to be a mother! But this was no joke. God was really going to give Abraham and Sarah a son. And from this one son, Abraham would become the father of many nations (Genesis 17:5).

What an amazing promise God gave to Abraham and Sarah while feasting with them in their home. As we read this story, we learn that God always keeps His promises. God always does what He says He will do. Remember to trust God and His Word.

Loving God, help me to remember that You always keep Your promises. Help me to remember that what You say in the Bible is true. Amen.

FAITH TO-GO

If three guests came to your home today, what would you serve them to eat?

SURVIVAL IN THE DESERT

GENESIS 21:8-21

Life had changed for Hagar and her son, Ishmael. They weren't welcome in their home anymore. They had to leave the only place they knew and find a brand new place to live. Life was going to be hard.

Hagar was worried about trying to survive in the desert. How would they get food? How would they get water? How would they be able to survive on their own?

When they left their old home, Abraham gave them some food and water. But in that hot climate, it didn't take long for them to drink all of the water. They were thirsty and had no idea where they would find more water in the desert.

GOD'S DAILY SPECIAL

"Then God opened her eyes and she saw a well of water. So she went and filled the skin with water and gave the boy a drink."
Genesis 21:19

Hagar began to cry, and so did Ishmael. They knew they could not survive for long without water. But guess who heard their cries? God! God told Hagar that He had heard their cry for help, and He told her not to be afraid.

And then, God provided.

When God opened Hagar's eyes, she could see a well of water! She was so excited, and she filled her jar to the top right away. She and Ishmael drank the water and were so happy. God had heard their cry for help, and He provided exactly what they needed.

You may never be stuck in the desert without food and water like Hagar and Ishmael, but you will probably be in lots of situations where you need something. When you find yourself in a situation like that, remember that God will provide what you need. Notice I didn't say He will provide what you want. Our needs are different from our wants, but God gives us exactly what we need when we need it. We can believe that because of how He provided for Hagar and Ishmael.

Lord, thank You for providing all I need to live. Help me to always thank You for everything You give to me. Amen.

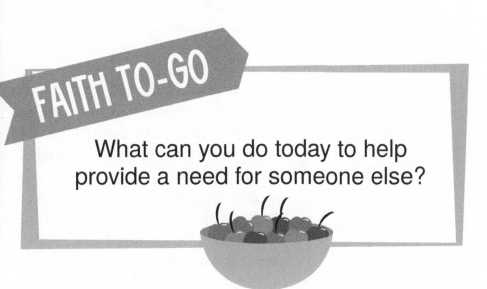

FAITH TO-GO

What can you do today to help provide a need for someone else?

JACOB GETS ESAU'S BLESSING

GENESIS 27:1-29

Do you like to eat game (which means hunted animals, like deer)? I am not a fan of deer meat, but my husband loves it!

A man in our Bible story today asked his son to prepare him a meal of game and tasty food. That man was Isaac.

Isaac was nearing the end of his life and it was time to give his oldest son, Esau, a special blessing. You see, firstborn sons in every family received this blessing. It was something that children wanted from their fathers, because they thought it would help them succeed in life. In this family, Esau was the oldest and Jacob was the youngest (they were actually twins, but Esau was born first). So Esau was set to receive this special blessing (which was like a powerful prayer spoken over him).

> ### GOD'S DAILY SPECIAL
>
> "Jacob said to his father, 'I am Esau your firstborn. I have done as you told me. Please sit up and eat some of my game, so that you may give me your blessing.'"
> Genesis 27:19

But Isaac wanted something tasty to eat before he blessed his son, so he asked Esau to go out and hunt an animal, then bring it back and prepare it for a meal.

While Esau was out hunting, Jacob and his mother, Rebekah, put together a plan to trick Isaac into giving Jacob the blessing meant for Esau. Isaac was blind, so they decided to cover Jacob with lots of hair. They thought this would trick Isaac into thinking Esau had returned, since Esau was a hairy man. Then, Rebekah prepared the meal Isaac had requested of Esau. Jacob, pretending to be Esau, served his dad the food and answered all the questions Isaac asked. Isaac wasn't sure at first if it was really Esau, but eventually, he fell for the trick and prayed that special blessing over Jacob, thinking he was his older brother.

Jacob and his mother didn't do the right thing that day. They wanted something so bad that they decided to lie to get what they wanted.

Is that what they should have done? No. And that's not how we should treat others, either. It's okay to have goals in your life, but you should never hurt other people to get what you want. They hurt Esau and Isaac that day.

Stay tuned for tomorrow's devotion, when we will find out exactly how Esau acted when he found out what Jacob had done.

Holy God, help me to always do the right thing. Give me wisdom to do what You want me to do. Forgive me when the things I do hurt others. Amen.

FAITH TO-GO

Today, treat a friend or family member the way you would want to be treated.

7

ESAU COMES FOR HIS BLESSING

GENESIS 27:30-40

How do you feel when someone you love does something to hurt you or takes away something that belongs to you?

My guess is that you are angry! You probably yell, scream, and maybe even cry. You can't understand why someone you love would hurt you on purpose.

That's exactly how Esau felt when he arrived home after he'd gone hunting for some food for his father.

Esau came back and prepared the meal for his dad (just like Isaac had asked). I can imagine he was super excited to give this meal to his father, because he knew the blessing he would receive was going to be awesome.

But his smile and excitement faded into an angry frown when he brought the meal to his dad. Imagine Esau's shock when his dad told him he had already blessed him! Esau knew that was impossible because he had been out hunting. He knew he had not yet received the blessing.

GOD'S DAILY SPECIAL

"When Esau heard his father's words, he burst out with a loud and bitter cry and said to his father, 'Bless me – me too, my father!'"
Genesis 27:34

Isaac, his dad, was also confused and upset. He had no idea who he had blessed. Esau began crying out for his dad to bless him. Then Isaac realized that his younger son, Jacob, had deceitfully stolen the blessing meant for Esau. Even worse, Isaac could not do anything about it.

You're probably thinking, "Why was Esau so upset about a blessing?" But here's the thing: once a blessing was spoken over someone it could not be reversed or spoken again over someone else. It was a one-time thing. Jacob had tricked his dad into thinking he was Esau, taking Esau's special blessing for himself. Esau cried and cried over this. He wanted a blessing, too, but now he could never have the special blessing meant for the firstborn son.

Esau was really angry at his brother, and Jacob feared for his life because of that. So Jacob ran away from home and lived far away for a long time. But guess what? Esau eventually forgave Jacob and they loved one another again.

It's hard to forgive someone, especially when they have hurt you. But God asks us to forgive one another just as He forgives us. It may take some time (like it did for Esau), but I pray you will be able to find it in your heart to forgive.

Father God, thank You for forgiving us of the wrong things that we do. Help me to forgive others as You forgive me. Amen.

FAITH TO-GO

Are there people you need to forgive? Make a list of people who have hurt you and whom you need to forgive. Ask God to help you show forgiveness to them.

FOOD TRUCK MENU

It's time to start the engine of your imagination! The first thing you need to do in creating your very own food truck ministry—one that will serve food and share the love of Jesus—is to figure out what kind of food you want to serve. Most food trucks serve a specific type of food. For example, I have seen taco food trucks (which serve a variety of tacos), burger food trucks (which serve a variety of burgers), bakery food trucks (which serve all kinds of desserts), and even ice cream food trucks (which serve all kinds of ice cream).

So take a minute to think about what type of food you want to serve. Write some of your ideas in the space below.

FOOD TRUCK MENU

GOT YOUR IDEA? NOW, COME UP WITH A MENU FOR YOUR FOOD TRUCK.
IN THE BOX BELOW, WRITE OUT A MENU. LIST FOODS AND PRICES.
DECORATE THE MENU BOARD IF YOU LIKE AS WELL!

JOSEPH SOLD INTO SLAVERY

GENESIS 37:12-33

How many of you argue a lot with your brothers or sisters? I would probably be right if I said that almost everyone fights with their siblings. Maybe you argue over who ate the last piece of pizza—especially if you already claimed it! Maybe you're upset because they won't let you play with one of their toys. Maybe you yell because they locked you out of their room. Maybe you fight because they called you a mean name. Maybe you get frustrated because it's your turn to play a video game and they won't let you. No matter how much you fight, I still know one thing: you love them. They are your friend and sibling, so even when you don't get along, you still love each other.

Joseph was one of twelve siblings. That's a lot, right? He wasn't the youngest, but he was one of the younger ones. Joseph liked to brag about things—like the dreams he had where his brothers did whatever Joseph said because he ruled over them.

Joseph's father loved him so much that he gave him a special colorful coat. Joseph liked to show that off, too, which made his brothers jealous.

Joseph's brothers did not like him AT ALL. In fact, they hated him so much that they plotted a way to get rid of him. They decided to strip his colorful coat off and throw him into a pit.

After they had done this mean thing to their brother, they sat down to eat a meal. While they were eating, they saw a caravan of

> ### GOD'S DAILY SPECIAL
>
> "As they sat down to eat their meal, they looked up and saw a caravan of Ishmaelites coming from Gilead."
> Genesis 37:25

Ishmaelites coming and they decided to sell Joseph to them! For 20 shekels, they handed over their little brother, Joseph.

Guess how much 20 shekels equals in US dollars? $6.25![2] That is not a lot of money at all! It's hard to believe that Joseph's brothers plotted to get rid of him while they ate a meal.

I never liked reading this story about Joseph being sold into slavery by his brothers. I wish they loved him instead of hating him. I wish they would have talked to him about their frustration instead of seeking out a way to get rid of him. But I do love the way the story ends. Joseph ends up being the governor of Egypt. Because he is in charge, he gets to help his brothers and their families during the bad famine that strikes their country. God works all things for good.

Is there something your brother or sister has done that has really made you mad or caused you to be so annoyed with them? If so, talk it out with them. Have a conversation. Hug each other. And then find a way to forgive each other.

Awesome God, I am sorry for saying things I should not say or doing things I should not do to my brother or sister. Help me to be kind and loving toward them from now on. In Jesus' name, Amen.

---

2 https://currencyconvert.net/israeli-shekel/dollar/20

FAITH TO-GO

At dinner, make a list with your family of ways you can encourage one another. What are things you can do to build each other up?

PHARAOH'S DREAM

GENESIS 41:15-32

Have you ever dreamed about food? Maybe you have. Maybe you dreamed about a food you liked, or maybe you dreamed about a food you really hated.

But have you ever had dreams about cows and grain? No? Me neither. But Pharaoh (the leader of Egypt) did have dreams about cows and grain, and he needed help figuring out what they meant.

GOD'S DAILY SPECIAL

"It is just as I said to Pharaoh: God has shown Pharaoh what he is about to do. Seven years of great abundance are coming throughout the land of Egypt, but seven years of famine will follow them."
Genesis 41:28-30

Pharaoh had heard from one of his servants about a man named Joseph (the same Joseph from our story yesterday) who could interpret dreams. So Pharaoh sent for Joseph and asked if he could explain his dreams about cows and grain.

When Pharaoh asked Joseph if he could interpret dreams, Joseph said, "I cannot do it, but God will give Pharaoh the answer he desires" (Genesis 41:16). Joseph made sure to tell Pharaoh that the interpretation he was about to give was not from him, but from God. He wanted to make sure Pharaoh knew that God was in this.

Pharaoh shared his really crazy dream with Joseph. He saw seven healthy cows, then seven unhealthy cows. The unhealthy cows ate the healthy cows. Then, in another dream, he saw seven heads of grain that were good and growing on one stalk. Then he saw seven thin heads of grain that were withered. The seven good heads were eaten by the seven withered heads of grain. Such a weird dream, right?

Joseph goes on to tell Pharaoh that the dreams about the cows and grain have the same meaning. The seven cows and seven heads of grain equal seven good years. The seven unhealthy cows and seven withered heads of grain equal seven years of famine (which means there will be no food for the people to eat during those years).

God was sending Pharaoh a message: be prepared. A famine is coming. God gave him a warning, and He expected Pharaoh to listen so that God's people would be taken care of during the famine.

God speaks to us in so many different ways: through the Bible, other people, books, worship music, and even our dreams. In this case, He sent two dreams about food to Pharaoh and then used Joseph to interpret them. God wanted to make sure the leader of Egypt heard His message and was prepared. How does God speak to you?

Loving God, help me to open my ears and listen for You every day. Amen.

FAITH TO-GO

How can you listen to God?

JOSEPH IN CHARGE OF EGYPT

GENESIS 41:41-49

What does your family do when a snowstorm is headed your way? Do your parents go to the grocery store to stock up on food? Maybe they buy bread, milk, eggs, and canned goods in case you are stuck at home and unable to get out for a while. We don't get snow very often where I live, so if snow is predicted, everyone rushes to the grocery store to get food just in case it might be a while before we can get out of the house again! (Yes, I live in the South!).

That's exactly what Joseph did in the land of Egypt.

Pharaoh made Joseph in charge of the land of Egypt. He was second-in-command in the whole country, and everyone listened to him.

Joseph remembered the dreams God gave Pharaoh and began stocking up on food. During the seven years of abundance (which means there was a lot of food), Joseph stored up all the food that grew in the land. In every city in Egypt, he stored up grain that had been grown in the fields surrounding that city. The Bible said Joseph stored up so much grain that he stopped counting how much he had!

GOD'S DAILY SPECIAL

"Joseph stored up huge quantities of grain, like the sand of the sea; it was so much that he stopped keeping records because it was beyond measure."
Genesis 41:49

Joseph did a fabulous job of storing up food, just as God told him and Pharaoh to do. Pharaoh listened to God and made Joseph in charge of everything. And Joseph listened to God by storing the grain so that when the famine came, everyone in the land would have enough to eat.

Joseph shared the food he stored up with all the people who lived in Egypt. God asks us to share our food with others, too. This could be with friends who don't have much, homeless people who live on the street, or even our neighbors who are going through a difficult time. Pray together as a family and ask God to show you how you can share your food with others.

Almighty God, help me to listen to You. Help me give food to others who are in need. In Jesus' name, Amen.

FAITH TO-GO

If you have food stored up at your home, how can you help share that with others?

11

THE FAMINE BEGINS

GENESIS 41:53-57

Have you ever heard of a food pantry? A food pantry is a place people can go when they do not have enough money to buy the food they need. The food pantry passes out food donated by the local community to feed people who need help. Many people are blessed by food pantries and by the generosity of those who are able to give extra food to them.

GOD'S DAILY SPECIAL

"And all the world came to Egypt to buy grain from Joseph, because the famine was severe everywhere."
Genesis 41:57

At this point in Joseph's story, the famine arrives. In most of the land, there was no food to be found. But one place had food, and that place was Egypt. Egypt had food because Joseph had listened to God and stored up plenty of grain over the past seven years.

When the famine started, Joseph opened all the storehouses that were filled with grain and sold it to the Egyptians. Word traveled fast! Soon, people from all around the world were coming to Egypt to buy grain to eat. The famine was so severe that it was affecting people everywhere, not just in Egypt. God used Joseph and Egypt to help feed the whole world. How cool is that!

God can use you to help feed others too! There are many people in our world who are without food. Many people live in countries who don't have enough food in their area. Even some people in your own city or state don't have anything to eat.

Here are some ways your family can feed those in need:

- Donate food (like canned goods) to your local food pantry.
- Volunteer to help pack food boxes at your local food pantry.
- Donate money to an organization that helps feed people in need.
- Help serve a hot meal at a soup kitchen.
- Sponsor a child in another country through World Vision or Compassion International.
- Pray for those who are hungry and ask God how you can help feed others.

God can use you and your family in big and small ways to help feed the hungry.

Loving God, show me how I can help those who are hungry. Please help those who are in need find something to eat. In Jesus' name, Amen.

FAITH TO-GO

Contact your local food pantry and ask how you can help them serve the hungry in your community.

12

LAND FLOWING WITH MILK & HONEY

EXODUS 3:1-10

I want you to think about all the places you've visited on family vacations or school field trips. Which one of them had the best food? I bet you'd like to visit that place again!

Maybe you're thinking of the fried shrimp you had at the beach, or the hamburger you ate while visiting your favorite amusement park. You could be remembering that ice cream sundae you had in the mountains, or the restaurant that serves your favorite macaroni and cheese. Yummy food can be found in a lot of cool places, big and small.

What if someone said you needed to go to a land flowing with milk and honey? Would that seem like a cool place to visit because of its food?

Maybe it wouldn't seem cool to us today, but for the people who lived in ancient Bible times, a land flowing with milk and honey was the best place ever! But this phrase not only means that the land had milk and honey, but it was used to mean that the land had an abundance of food. To say it was a land flowing with milk and honey meant that it would be a place you would want to live because it had great sources of food!

> ### GOD'S DAILY SPECIAL
>
> "So I have come down to rescue them from the hand of the Egyptians and to bring them up out of that land into a good and spacious land, a land flowing with milk and honey – the home of the Canaanites, Hittites, Amorites, Perizzites, Hivites and Jebusites."
> Exodus 3:8

In our Bible story today, we find God speaking to Moses through a burning bush. That is pretty awesome! God tells Moses He will use him to lead the Israelites out of slavery and into the Promised Land, which is the land flowing with milk and honey that we've been talking about.

During the famine in the reign of Joseph, many people came to live in Egypt because the country had food. But after Joseph died, those in charge after him didn't like the Israelites, because there were so many of them. So God's people became slaves in the land and had to work for food to survive. It was a hard life for the Israelites, and they cried out to God to save them! God heard their cries and told Moses to convince Pharaoh to let His people go.

If you need God's help with something in your life, cry out to Him. Ask Him to guide you and use His strength to overcome whatever you are going through. God hears you, just like He heard the Israelites cry for help, and He will answer you.

Dear Lord, thank You for always taking care of me. Hear my cry today and help me overcome what is going on. I love You, God. Amen.

FAITH TO-GO

How can you use milk and honey
to help someone today?

13

QUAIL AND MANNA FROM HEAVEN

EXODUS 16:1-16

What is it?

You may have asked your parents that question before as you saw what was on the plate of food they handed you. You might have wondered why they placed a strange thing on your plate for you to eat. Maybe whatever it was didn't look too appetizing, either.

That's exactly what the Israelites said to God when He gave them food to eat in the middle of nowhere.

GOD'S DAILY SPECIAL

"The Lord said to Moses, 'I have heard the grumbling of the Israelites. Tell them, 'At twilight you will eat meat, and in the morning you will be filled with bread. Then you will know that I am the Lord your God.'"
Exodus 16:11-12

God called Moses to lead the Israelites out of Egypt. He led them safely out into the wilderness. But the Israelites were hungry! They wanted some food to eat, and they began complaining to Moses about it.

God heard their complaining and sent them food to eat. He told them that He would give them meat to eat every night and bread to eat every morning.

That first evening, quail came down from heaven and covered their camp. The meat had arrived, and they were so glad!

The next morning when they woke up, all they saw was a layer of dew around the camp. Once the dew was gone, all that was left was *something* that looked like frost on the ground. They were a little confused. God said He would give them bread, but instead, all they saw was this flaky substance. And they said to each other, "What is it?" (Exodus 16:15). They really had no clue what this stuff on the ground was.

Moses had to clear up the confusion for the Israelites. He told them this flaky substance on the ground was the bread that God had promised. Hmm… they still might have been confused because they had never seen bread like that before! But they collected what they needed. God told them to take an omer for each person in their tent. (An omer is around 3 pounds.)

God knew what they needed to eat. He provided them with food that would fill their bellies and make them feel satisfied. It might not have been the food they were used to eating while living in Egypt, but God provided the food they needed every single day while they were in the wilderness.

God is so good to give us what we need. Just as He gave the Israelites food they needed, He will give you and your family the food you need as well.

Thank You, God, for providing food that I need to live on. Help me to always be thankful for what I have to eat. Amen.

FAITH TO-GO

Eat something new today and be thankful!

14

THE FOOD GOES BAD

EXODUS 16:17-20

I have a friend who went to the grocery store and bought some hamburger meat, along with other non-food items. She brought all the items home and put them away. She tucked the non-food items she bought under her bed because they were Christmas presents.

A few days later, she began smelling something really bad in her house. It smelled like a dead mouse. She couldn't figure out where the smell was coming from, but it was strongest in her bedroom. She began looking all over her bedroom to figure out where the smell was coming from. She pulled out the bags of items she bought the other day from the store, and she found the source of the horrible smell! She had accidentally left the hamburger meat in the bag with the Christmas presents from the store several days before. The hamburger meat had gone bad and made her whole house smell terrible!

> ### GOD'S DAILY SPECIAL
>
> "Then Moses said to them, 'No one is to keep any of it until morning.'"
> Exodus 16:19

Food that has gone bad (like left out hamburger meat) smells awful. You can't cook it because it would not be safe to eat. You just have to throw it away.

God told the Israelites to collect just enough manna in the morning to last for one day for their family. God specifically told the Israelites they were to eat all the manna they collected by the end of the day instead of saving it for tomorrow's meals. (Every day, God gave them new manna to eat, so they didn't need to save it for the next day.)

But guess what?

Some people didn't listen to God. They saved some extra manna for the next day. Do you know what happened to it? It became "full of maggots and began to smell" (Exodus 16:20). Gross! Their bread had bugs in it, and it made their tents smell so bad! They could not eat it and they had to throw it out. That manna was wasted food.

God was unhappy with the Israelites because they did not follow His instructions. They decided to disobey what God had told them and did what they wanted to do instead. It turned out to be a big, gross mistake.

Sometimes we think we know everything. Sometimes we think we know what's best for us. Sometimes we may even think we know more than God. But do we really? No, we don't—and that's where our faith comes in. We have to trust God and believe He knows what is best for us. We must follow Him closely and do all that He tells us (which means we need to read our Bible to know what He says.) When we follow Him closely, we can be sure that He will give us all we need.

Father God, help me to listen to all You ask of me. Help me to trust in You with all my heart. In Jesus' name, Amen.

FAITH TO-GO

If you have leftover food at the end of the day, deliver to friends in need or to a homeless shelter.

FOOD TRUCK NAME & LOGO

You have your menu and the type of food you want to serve. Now you need a name and a logo!

Brainstorm names and write several of them in the space below.

FOOD TRUCK LOGO

INSIDE THE CIRCLE, DRAW A LOGO FOR YOUR FOOD TRUCK USING THE NAME YOU HAVE CHOSEN.

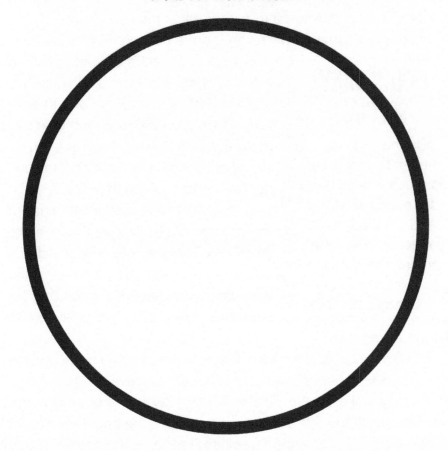

15

FOOD ON THE SABBATH DAY

EXODUS 16:21-26

Did you know that God commands us to rest? In the Ten Commandments, God actually says for us to keep the Sabbath (which is a day of rest). On this day, we take a break from all our work.

In today's story, we are back with the Israelites. Remember, God has given them manna and quail to eat, and He's also told them to collect just what they need to eat for each day.

Now we see that God's given them a new command, too: He's told them to collect a double portion on the sixth day, two omers for each person instead of one. (That would equal around six pounds of manna.) God gave them this rule because the seventh day was made for resting—and that includes not baking or cooking their food!

I can just imagine what was going through the minds of the Israelites when God told them to collect a double portion on the sixth day. I am sure they were confused, because when they had collected more manna than they needed before, it went bad!

> ## GOD'S DAILY SPECIAL
>
> "On the sixth day, they gathered twice as much – two omers for each person – and the leaders of the community came and reported this to Moses."
> Exodus 16:22

But God showed them His miracle power. On the sixth day, they listened to His instructions and collected twice as much manna. When they woke up the next morning, they found out the manna was still good! The leftover manna had not gone bad after all!

What do you think the Israelites had to do on the sixth day? They had to prepare all their food for the next day (the seventh day). They had to think ahead and bake what was needed so their families could eat on the Sabbath day. Then, on the Sabbath, they could rest from their daily work (without worrying about cooking), and they also could spend time with God.

Have you ever tried resting one day and not doing anything? If you have, you probably found out that it's hard to do. That's because resting requires preparation. If you want to take a day of rest, you'll have to finish your homework ahead of time. If you want to take a day of rest in the kitchen, your parents may have to cook a meal the day before so there is no baking or cooking on the Sabbath. When we prepare ahead and get all our work done in six days, we can enjoy our day of rest and spend our time worshiping God and drawing closer to Him.

Creator God, thank You for giving us a day of rest. Help me to use one day of my week to rest and focus on You. In Jesus' name, Amen.

FAITH TO-GO

As a family, try doing what the Israelites did…cooking enough food on the sixth day so you don't have to cook on the seventh day and can enjoy a day of rest.

16

MANNA IN A JAR

EXODUS 16:31-36

Do your parents or grandparents "can" food? When someone cans their food, the food gets preserved so it will last for a long time. My great aunt used to can her own jelly. She always had tons of jars of red plum jelly in her pantry. I was glad when she shared it with our family, too. It was the best jelly!

God told Moses and Aaron to do the same thing. He wanted them to can some of the manna. That seems a little odd, right?

GOD'S DAILY SPECIAL

"Moses said, 'This is what the Lord has commanded: Take an omer of manna and keep it for the generations to come, so they can see the bread I gave you to eat in the wilderness when I brought you out of Egypt.'"
Exodus 16:32

Why would God ask Moses and Aaron to keep some of the manna in a jar? Why not just eat it?

God explains why in the Bible verse for today! The Israelites were to keep a small amount of manna in a jar so that generations to come would be reminded of how God provided for their people in the wilderness. It would remind them of all the stories we've talked about, including how God rescued them from slavery in Egypt and how He led them on a path to the Promised Land. It would remind them that God provided for them, giving them food to eat every day.

However, God knew that somewhere along the way, the Israelites would forget what He had done for them. Some parents would forget to tell their kids or grandkids or great-grandkids or great-great grandkids how God had provided for them. So God told Moses to put this jar of manna in the Ark of the Covenant (where the Ten Commandments was kept and where God's presence could be found). When anyone saw it, they would be reminded of how God provided for them.

How can you remember what God has done for you? It's important to remind ourselves of how good God is and how well He takes care of us. Maybe you could write it in a journal, draw a picture to hang in your bedroom, or maybe even wear a bracelet or necklace that helps you praise God for what He has done. All of these things can be used as a way to remember God. And when you see that thing, thank God for providing for you.

Heavenly Father, help me to always remember to give You thanks for the ways in which You provide for me. Amen.

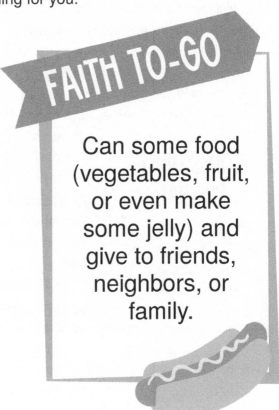

FAITH TO-GO

Can some food (vegetables, fruit, or even make some jelly) and give to friends, neighbors, or family.

17

THREE FESTIVALS

EXODUS 23:14-19

Have you ever been to a festival? There are all kinds of festivals, like arts & crafts festivals, music festivals, and fairs! Can you guess my favorite part about festivals?

The food!

I can always count on finding yummy food there. I know there will be stands with things like hamburgers, turkey legs, fried Oreos, funnel cakes, caramel apples, ice cream, and popsicles. I can't attend a festival without getting myself one of these treats!

> ### GOD'S DAILY SPECIAL
>
> "Three times a year you are to celebrate a festival to me."
> Exodus 23:14

Did you know God told the Israelites to celebrate three festivals every year? And they were all festivals centered around food. Now that's my kind of festival!

In Exodus 23, we find Moses teaching the Israelites all that God has shared with him. Earlier, God had sent Moses to the top of Mount Sinai, where He gave him the Ten Commandments. God also gave him laws for the people of Israel to live by.

Celebrating these three festivals was one of the laws God gave the Israelites to follow. Let's take a look at these festivals and see if the food seems appetizing to you...

First, we read about the Festival of Unleavened Bread. Think about bread with no yeast in it, which makes it flat. That's the kind of bread they were supposed to eat during this festival. God asked them to celebrate this festival for seven days and eat unleavened bread during this time. "Why?" you might be asking. Because this bread would remind them of how God rescued them from slavery in Egypt! Remember the manna?

The second festival was the Festival of Harvest (also known as the Feast of Weeks or Pentecost). During this festival, the Israelites were to bring the firstfruits of their fields to the temple. That means the first grain they harvested was offered to God at the temple. (See Leviticus 23 for more details).

The third festival was the Festival of Ingathering (also known as the Feast of Tabernacles or the Festival of Booths). This festival took place at the end of the year when the Israelites would gather all their crops from their fields. They would bring offerings to the Lord from their fruits, vegetables, and grains. They would also live in tents (booths) for seven days. This festival reminded them of leaving Egypt and depending on God to lead them and feed them in the wilderness.

Do you think God wanted them to remember what He had done for them by bringing them out of Egypt into the Promised Land? He did! And these three festivals were ways they could honor and obey God and remember Him.

How can you remember God today?

Heavenly Father, thank You for the Bible and how it teaches me how to live my life for You. Help me to honor You in all that I do. Amen.

FAITH TO-GO

If your city hosts a festival, set up a booth and pass out free water and snacks to people who attend. Remind them that God loves them.

18

MOSES FASTS ON MOUNT SINAI

EXODUS 34:1-28

Moses had to be hungry. It had been forty days and forty nights since he had anything to eat or drink. That's a long time to go without food and water!

But Moses spent those forty days and nights on Mount Sinai fasting (which means going without food) because he was spending that time with God. It was a very important time with God, too.

Let's back up just a little bit...

GOD'S DAILY SPECIAL

"Moses was there with the Lord forty days and forty nights without eating bread or drinking water. And he wrote on the tablets the words of the covenant – the Ten Commandments."
Exodus 34:28

Earlier, Moses had gone up to Mount Sinai and spent forty days with God while He gave him the Ten Commandments. Moses wrote these commandments down on stone tablets. During this time, the Israelites were getting impatient. They didn't know where their leader was or why he had been gone for so long. So they got Aaron (Moses's brother and the priest) to make a golden calf out of their jewelry. They wanted to worship it as a god, since they felt like God and Moses had abandoned them.

When Moses came off the mountain after forty days and found the Israelites worshiping the golden calf, he was furious (and so was God)! He was so mad that he took the stone tablets he had just used to write down the Ten Commandments and threw them on the ground. He threw them so hard that they broke into pieces! Moses also destroyed the golden calf and had a serious talk with Aaron and all the Israelites. He couldn't believe the horrible sin they had committed by worshiping another god.

Since he'd broken the stone tablets that the Ten Commandments were on, God asked Moses to come back up to Mount Sinai and spend forty more days with Him. God gave Moses the Ten Commandments again and had him write them down on new stone tablets.

This time, Moses decided to fast while he was on Mount Sinai with God. When we fast, we give up something as a way to draw closer to God. Moses needed this time alone with God so God could help him lead the Israelites.

We can't give up food for that long now, but we can give up *one* food that we love to eat for forty days as a way of drawing closer to God. You may have heard of Lent (a church season that is forty days before Easter). During this time, we may choose to give up a food or two that we love so we can draw closer to God, just like Moses did.

Holy God, help me to give up a food I love so that I can focus on my love for You. May I use this time to draw closer to You, just like Moses did. Amen.

FAITH TO-GO

What is one food you love that you can give up for the next forty days as a way to draw closer to God?

19

FOOD FOR THE POOR

LEVITICUS 19:9-10

Do you remember the COVID-19 pandemic that began in 2020? I know, it's hard to forget. Do you know what crazy thing I remember about the beginning of the pandemic? There was hardly any food at the grocery store (and no one had any toilet paper, hand sanitizer, or wipes either!). People were afraid of this virus and how it would affect them, so they went to the store and purchased a lot of food and other supplies, just in case they couldn't go back out for a while. It was a scary time.

> ## GOD'S DAILY SPECIAL
>
> "Do not go over your vineyard a second time or pick up the grapes that have fallen. Leave them for the poor and the foreigner. I am the Lord your God."
> Leviticus 19:10

This pandemic reminds me of the Bible verses we just read today in Leviticus 19. God is telling the Israelites what to do when they are harvesting their crops. I've never harvested a crop, but I can imagine you would want to make sure to gather everything you'd grown from your field. You definitely wouldn't want to leave any good crops in the field. You would harvest them all!

But God told the Israelites to do something different.

God told them not to collect everything. He says, "Do not reap to the very edges of your field or gather the gleanings of your harvest" (Leviticus 19:9). He also told them not to go over their field a second time to make sure they got everything, but instead, to leave anything they missed behind.

Why would God tell them to leave good crops on the field? He wanted them to leave some food for the poor.

God asked them not to harvest all the crops because there were people in their community who could not afford to buy food to eat. God asked the Israelites to leave some food for those who had none.

During the COVID-19 pandemic, stores limited the number of items you could buy. They set this limit to make sure everyone had enough food to eat (and enough toilet paper to use). Food and supplies were flying off the shelves fast! If those stores hadn't put a limit on the number of items you could buy, we all would have been without food.

God wants all His children to be fed and not to go hungry. God uses those who have more to give to those who have less. I am thankful for this.

Giving God, help me to give food to those who are in need. Show me how You can use me to help feed those who have none. In Jesus' name, Amen.

FAITH TO-GO

Instead of going out to eat for a meal, use that money to buy food needed to help feed the poor.

20

EXPLORING THE LAND OF CANAAN

NUMBERS 13:17-25

Have you ever had to move to a different city, state, or country? If you have, why did you move there? Was it because one of your parents got a new job? Maybe your family bought a home in a new area. Or maybe you moved to live closer to family. There are lots of reasons why you might have moved.

Have you ever moved to a new city because of the food that was available there? That's one of the reasons God was leading the Israelites to the Promised Land. God said it was a land flowing with milk and honey (which meant it had good soil and good land to grow crops).

> ## GOD'S DAILY SPECIAL
>
> "'Do your best to bring back some of the fruit of the land.' (It was the season for the first ripe grapes.)"
> Numbers 13:20

In our Bible story in Numbers 13, we find the Israelites still wandering around in the wilderness. They haven't made it to the Promised Land yet (also known as the land of Canaan). But they were getting closer, so it was time to go spy out the land to see what kind of food was there.

God told Moses to send some men to explore the new land. Moses chose twelve men, one from each tribe, and sent them on their way. Moses asked the men to look for a few specific things. He wanted to know how strong the people were, how many people lived there, what kind of towns they lived in, if the cities had walls or not, how good the soil was, and if there were trees in the land. Lastly, he asked them to bring back some of the land's fruit (see Numbers 13:17-20).

So the men set off to explore Canaan and search for the answers to Moses's questions. They spent the next forty days on a mission.

Do you think the men found some good food in the land? Yes, they did! They found grapes, pomegranates, and figs. Yummy! I bet they enjoyed sampling the food while they were exploring, and they probably loved having full bellies while they were away on their mission, too! When they had the answers they needed, these twelve spies packed up the food and headed back home to report their knowledge of the land to Moses.

How does God want you to explore? Is He asking you to read your Bible more so you can know more about Him? Does He want you to spend time with Him every day? Is He wanting you to pray more? Could He be asking you to put others' needs before your own? Think and pray about how you can explore more of your relationship with God so you can be closer to Him.

Father God, help me to hear how You want me to explore more about You. Show me the way I should go and help me to obey. In Jesus' name, Amen.

FAITH TO-GO

Pick a book of the Bible and begin reading one chapter daily.

21

THE REPORT ON THE LAND

NUMBERS 13:26-33

The twelve spies that explored the land of Canaan for Moses came back to their camp after forty days. They had collected a lot of information and food, and they couldn't wait to share all about it. They showed Moses the food they had brought back and told him that what God said was true. It really was a land flowing with milk and honey!

But somehow, finding good food was not enough to stir up excitement about moving to the land of Canaan. The men said the Israelites were not as strong as the people who already lived in the land. Even worse, the spies said that the cities in the land of Canaan were large and were well protected by walls and forts. Even though the food was amazing, they were scared of the people and their cities. The spies didn't think they had what it would take to move into their land and take over it.

But two of the explorers, Caleb and Joshua, disagreed with all the other men. They had a different outlook on the land and knew the Israelites could live there. Why? Because they believed what God said. They believed the power of God would help the Israelites overtake the people living in Canaan and move into the Promised Land.

But it didn't matter what Caleb and Joshua thought. All the other men went back to their tribes and told everyone that the land was good, but the people and the cities were too big for the Israelites

GOD'S DAILY SPECIAL

"Then Caleb silenced the people before Moses and said, 'We should go up and take possession of the land, for we can certainly do it.'"
Numbers 13:30

to fight. They even compared themselves to grasshoppers (which means the Israelites must have felt tiny compared to the Canaanites)! They really did not give a good report to Moses and the other Israelites.

What can we learn from this story? Like Caleb and Joshua, we can learn to trust God even when things look way too big for us to handle. God had given this land to the Israelites, but they didn't listen to Him when He said He would be with them. Remember that God is with you, and He will always do what He promises.

Loving God, remind me today of Your presence with me. Help me to trust in You even when I am scared. Amen.

FAITH TO-GO

Write a letter of thanks to your local mayor or county commissioner sharing with them all the things you love about the town you live in. Thank them for helping make your town a great place to live!

FOOD TRUCK BIBLE VERSE

Your food truck ministry needs to be centered around a Bible verse.

In the space below, write out several Scripture verses you might like to use for your food truck ministry.

FOOD TRUCK
BIBLE VERSE

IN THE BOX BELOW, WRITE IN THE BIBLE VERSE YOU HAVE CHOSEN TO USE FOR YOUR FOOD TRUCK.

22

NOT LIVING ON BREAD ALONE

DEUTERONOMY 8:3

How can you stand eating the same thing every day?

That's what a friend said to me one day. You see, I had to have my gallbladder removed. Now, to keep my stomach from hurting, I only eat certain foods that won't upset my stomach. I could go back to eating lots of fried foods, bread, and ice cream, but I would feel really sick afterwards. I don't like being sick, so I found a way of eating. I do eat a variety of foods, but to my friends, sometimes it seems like I eat the same foods every day. Does it get old? Yes, but I am very thankful that it helps my stomach!

The question my friend asked me is the same thing I would have liked to have asked the Israelites. How could they have enjoyed eating the same thing every day? Wouldn't it get old to eat manna and quail every single day for forty years?

In today's verse, we find Moses telling the Israelites not to forget the Lord. They have made it through forty years in the wilderness, and it's finally time to claim God's promise, which is the land of Canaan. But before they do, Moses wants to remind them of all God has provided for them.

GOD'S DAILY SPECIAL

"He humbled you, causing you to hunger and then feeding you with manna, which neither you nor your ancestors had known, to teach you that man does not live on bread alone but on every word that comes from the mouth of the Lord."
Deuteronomy 8:3

Every day for forty years, God gave the Israelites their food. He provided them with manna and quail. All they had to do was collect their food and cook it. It probably wasn't what they would have chosen to eat, but God's provision kept their stomachs full for all those years. Moses wanted to make sure the people remembered that.

In Deuteronomy 8:3, Moses says, "man does not live on bread alone but on every word that comes from the mouth of the Lord." This means the Israelites did not survive just by eating their manna and quail every day. Yes, God provided the daily bread they needed for their physical health, but even more than that, He was teaching them to trust in Him. They survived by remembering God, being thankful, and being obedient to Him.

The same applies to us today. We live on the food God provides for us, but we also live on His Word, the Bible. We read the Bible to discover more and more about God, which helps us grow deeper in our faith in Him.

So get that Bible out! Read it and discover God's great love for you.

Holy God, thank You for the Bible. Help me to read it every day so I can learn more about You. Amen.

FAITH TO-GO

Read the Bible and play Bingo at the same time! Check out the different Bible Bingo games found on my website: www.vanessamyers.org

23

CLEAN AND UNCLEAN FOOD

DEUTERONOMY 14:1-21

Have you ever wondered why there are certain animals we eat and certain animals we don't eat? Why can we eat chicken all the time, but we never eat other birds like eagles and falcons?

Maybe you've never thought about this, but in the Old Testament (which was written before Jesus was born on the earth), God gave His people laws to live by. Some of these laws were about clean and unclean foods. Sounds a little odd, right? Why would God give a law about what His people can and can't eat?

GOD'S DAILY SPECIAL

"But you are a people holy to the Lord your God."
Deuteronomy 14:21

As I dug deeper into this Scripture passage from Deuteronomy 14, I read several articles that shared the main reason why God made laws about what foods to eat. The reason: God called His people to be holy, just as He is holy.

It actually says so, right there in Deuteronomy 14:2, "Out of all the peoples on the face of the earth, the Lord has chosen you to be his treasured possession." God called the Israelites to live a holy life, and part of that holy life was to eat only the foods that were considered clean. God loved them and wanted them to be holy, just as He was.

I believe God also created these laws about food to keep His people safe. If they ate unclean animals, they would get sick. Think about it this way: what would happen if you ate food that you shouldn't eat, or if you ate *a lot* of one food? You would probably get sick, and that's not any fun. I believe God wanted to make sure His people were safe, and that meant telling them what they could and couldn't eat.

We can relate this story to our lives today by eating well, which means eating foods we know are good for us, eating smaller portions of food, and being healthy people. God wants us to take care of our bodies, and that means eating healthy whenever we can. I'm working on doing this for my own health. Will you join me? Let's be holy as God is holy and eat well!

Loving God, help me to eat foods that are good for me. I know it will be hard to do, so I ask for Your strength in eating right. Amen.

FAITH TO-GO

Make a list of healthy foods you can start eating.

24

FIRSTFRUITS OF THE LAND

DEUTERONOMY 26:1-4

Have you ever given an offering at church? You may like to put in a few coins or a dollar bill as the plate is passed down your row. Taking an offering at church is our way of giving back to God. We give our money to our local church, and then the church uses it to do God's work in our community and our world.

In the Old Testament, people gave an offering to God, too, but God asked them to give something different than money. He asked them to offer the firstfruits from their land. Firstfruits? That's a new word for most of us, I bet.

GOD'S DAILY SPECIAL

"Take some of the firstfruits of all that you produce from the soil of the land the Lord your God is giving you and put them in a basket."
Deuteronomy 26:2

Firstfruits are the very first pieces of produce (or food) someone harvests from their crops. Think about someone who grows grain (wheat, barley, or rice). When the people who farmed grain in the Old Testament harvested their crop each year, they took the very first grain they harvested and brought it to the priest, who then gave it as an offering to God. That's how God asked them to honor Him.

It's different from the way we honor God today, right? But their firstfruit offering was a way for them to remember all God had done for them by bringing them out of slavery in Egypt and leading them to the Promised Land, where they could have land, grow food, and worship Him.

Today, God asks us to give money as an offering to Him, but we still give our firstfruits in a way! This means that when we get paid for the work we do, we give the first of that money to the Lord. We don't pay bills or spend that money on shopping or groceries first. We give that money back to God by giving to the church or to another ministry.

So what can you do as a kid to give an offering to God? If you get an allowance, give 10% of it (which is called a tithe) to God by putting it in the offering plate at church. For example, if you get $10.00 as an allowance, you would give $1.00 as an offering to God.

Let's honor God by giving our offerings (or firstfruits) to Him!

Giving God, help me to honor You by giving an offering to You. Show me other ways I can honor You, too. Amen.

FAITH TO-GO

If you had a farm, what would you grow? List ways you could give the firstfruits of your crops to God. Where could you donate your crops to?

25

THE MANNA ENDS

JOSHUA 5:10-12

Pretend you are an Israelite for a minute…

The day has finally come. It's a day that seemed to take forever to get here (actually, it took 40 years, so it did take forever). But it's a day you will never forget. This is a day you will tell your grandchildren and great-grandchildren about. It's an epic day!

So what kind of day is it?

It's the day when the manna stopped (cue the party music here!). You are so excited because you don't have to eat any more manna! Forty years of manna was a long time! It's a happy day!

GOD'S DAILY SPECIAL

"The manna stopped the day after they ate this food from the land; there was no longer any manna for the Israelites, but that year they ate the produce of Canaan."
Joshua 5:12

In the book of Joshua, we read about this happy day when it was finally time for the Israelites to cross over into the Promised Land. God told Joshua to lead the Israelites across the Jordan River. God parted the waters and they walked across, then finally stepped foot onto the land that would be their new home—the home God had promised them forty years before.

God also asked them to collect twelve stones out of the Jordan River as they crossed. They set them up as a memorial at Gilgal (their camp) so they would always remember how God kept His promise to them.

When they entered the Promised Land, they no longer needed the manna and quail God had provided every day for the past forty years. They didn't need it because (if you remember) this was a land flowing with milk and honey! It was a fruitful land filled with many different types of food, and God told them it was all theirs to eat.

When they settled into camp, they celebrated the Passover (a meal meant to remind them of the day God saved them and brought them out of Egypt). The day after Passover, they ate some food from the land.

What do you think they ate? Hamburger? Steak? Shrimp? Maybe that's what you would have liked to have eaten, but they actually ate unleavened bread (bread with no yeast so it was flat) and roasted grains. It was a glorious day of eating something totally different than manna or quail! I can just imagine the smiles on their faces. Maybe they even danced and celebrated when they ate these new things!

God is so good. He always follows through on His promises. The Israelites had finally arrived in the Promised Land, and they got to eat delicious food from their new homeland. Praise the Lord!

Holy God, thank You for keeping Your promises. Help me to be patient and focus on You while I wait. Amen.

FAITH TO-GO

Try a new food today! Then share that food with someone else.

26

GIDEON IS ENCOURAGED BY BREAD

JUDGES 7:7-16

Have you ever been afraid to do something? I think we could all answer, "Yes!" to that question. Maybe you're afraid to talk to someone you don't know, afraid to play in your soccer game, afraid to take a test at school, or afraid to go to the doctor. Lots of things might cause you to be afraid.

In our Bible story today, we meet a man named Gideon. He was called by God to fight the Midianites (they were the "bad guys" in this story). But Gideon had one problem: he was afraid. He wasn't sure why God chose him to lead the soldiers in their fight against these people. He kept asking God, "Are you sure you have the right man for the job?" Gideon didn't think he could do it because he was afraid.

GOD'S DAILY SPECIAL

"When Gideon heard the dream and its interpretation, he bowed down and worshiped."
Judges 7:15

God knew Gideon was afraid, so He gave him some directions. God said, "If you are afraid to attack, go down to the camp with your servant Purah and listen to what they are saying. Afterward, you will be encouraged to attack the camp" (Judges 7:10-11). I can just imagine the look on Gideon's face when God told him to go to the enemy's camp! He probably was even more afraid!

But Gideon did what God asked, and what he heard was truly encouraging! Just as he and his servant arrived, they overheard one of the Midianites share a dream he'd just woken up from. He dreamed that "a round loaf of barley bread came tumbling into the Midianite camp. It struck the tent with such force that the tent overturned and collapsed" (Judges 7:13). Another Midianite said that this loaf of bread represented the sword of Gideon, and that God had given the Midianites into his hands.

Wow, that is some amazing encouragement! And all because a man dreamed about bread! God used a dream about a loaf of bread to show Gideon that he was chosen to defeat the Midianites.

After this, Gideon was confident that he could do it with God's power helping him, and he boldly led the fight against the Midianites. And guess what? He defeated them!

Think back to that thing you might be afraid to do right now. Ask God to give you the same boldness and confidence He gave Gideon. Then, go out and do it!

Powerful God, thank You for how You used something as simple as bread to encourage Gideon. Help me to have confidence in what You ask me to do. Amen.

FAITH TO-GO

Make a loaf of your favorite bread
and deliver it to a friend.

27

RUTH GATHERS GRAIN

RUTH 2:1-13

Have you ever heard the word "gleaning?" You'll usually hear this word mentioned in conversations about farming or crops. To glean means to gather or collect what's left in the fields after the crops have been harvested. Basically, gleaning is like picking up the leftovers that the workers missed as they gathered the crops.

In our Bible story today, we find Ruth asking her mother-in-law, Naomi, if she can glean the fields. But let's back up: who are Ruth and Naomi? Well, Ruth married Naomi's son. But he died (along with the rest of Naomi's family), and Naomi was ready to move back home to Bethlehem (they had lived in Moab for a while because of a shortage of food in Bethlehem). Ruth decided to move back with her.

GOD'S DAILY SPECIAL

"And Ruth the Moabite said to Naomi, 'Let me go to the fields and pick up the leftover grain behind anyone in whose eyes I find favor.'"
Ruth 2:2

After they moved, Ruth wanted to gather some food for them so they could eat. She asked Naomi if she could "go to the fields and pick up the leftover grain behind anyone in whose eyes I find favor" (Ruth 2:2). Naomi told her to go. So off Ruth went to begin gleaning the grain in the fields in Bethlehem.

When Boaz arrived home, he noticed a new woman working in his field. He wondered who she was, and when he found out she was a relative of Naomi, he invited her to come back every day. He showed her kindness and hospitality. He told her not to go to anyone else's fields and let her know that she could come to his fields any time she needed food.

Boaz made Ruth feel very welcome. He took care of her and made sure she had all she needed. He ensured that Ruth and Naomi had enough grain to cook with, so they could be full. Boaz was truly kind to Ruth (and to Naomi).

Can you think of someone who has welcomed you and made you feel like part of their family? Maybe it was a teacher, a friend at school, a pastor, or a Sunday school teacher. Why do you think they showed you God's love and welcomed you? Because that's what God calls us to do. He teaches us to love others just as He does, and He shows us how to offer that same compassion to others so they feel welcome, too.

Holy God, thank You for teaching me how to love and welcome others. Thank You for the way I learn how to do that by reading Your Word. Show me who I can welcome today. In Jesus' name, Amen.

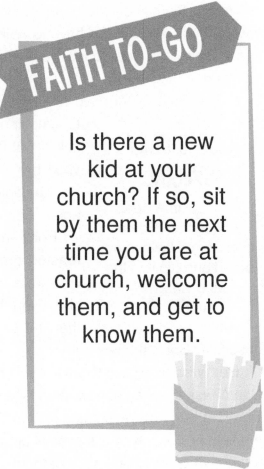

FAITH TO-GO

Is there a new kid at your church? If so, sit by them the next time you are at church, welcome them, and get to know them.

28

RUTH EATS A MEAL WITH BOAZ

RUTH 2:14-23

When I was in college, I did not like going to the Dining Hall (or what we called the Chow Hall) by myself to eat a meal. I usually had lots of friends to sit with, but sometimes my friends were out of town or busy, and I would have to walk to the Chow Hall by myself, find a table, and eat alone. I really hated those nights because I didn't like eating alone.

I think Ruth might have felt the same way when it came time to eat dinner after gleaning in Boaz's fields. But Boaz took care of this and invited her to have a meal with him and his harvesters. He was so welcoming and caring!

> ### GOD'S DAILY SPECIAL
> "At mealtime Boaz said to her, 'Come over here. Have some bread and dip it in the wine vinegar.'"
> Ruth 2:14

Boaz invited her to eat bread and roasted grain with him and the others who were harvesting. So Ruth ate, and she even had leftovers! She was so thankful for the bread, the grain and the hospitality Boaz showed her.

Ruth was so excited to tell Naomi how much grain she gathered. Naomi was shocked at how much she was able to glean and asked who had been so welcoming to her. When Ruth said she went to the field of Boaz, Naomi's eyes lit up, because she knew he was a relative who would take care of them.

From that point on, Boaz did take care of them. He protected Ruth by telling her only to glean from his fields (as she might get hurt or in trouble if she gleaned in anyone else's fields). Eventually, Boaz and Ruth got married. Guess who their great-grandson is? King David! And guess who is in the family tree of King David and Ruth? Jesus!

So Ruth, the poor woman who gathered leftover grain, went on to be in the family tree of Jesus, all because Boaz took care of her. He welcomed her into his fields. He watched out for her. He protected her. And he loved her.

Do you know who loves you even more than Boaz loved Ruth? Jesus. He loves you so much. And He longs for you to follow Him closely and love others the way He loves you.

Loving God, thank You for loving me. Help me to love others the way You love me. Amen.

FAITH TO-GO

Invite a friend over to have a meal with you and your family.

FOOD TRUCK MISSION STATEMENT

Every church, organization, or business has a mission statement. This statement is the purpose or the reason behind why they do what they do. So think about this...why are you starting your food truck? Who do you want to serve? Why are you helping people?

In the space below, write down the reasons why you are starting this food truck ministry.

FOOD TRUCK MISSION STATEMENT

IN THE BOX BELOW, WRITE OUT THE MISSION STATEMENT FOR YOUR FOOD TRUCK MINISTRY.

29

HANNAH DOESN'T EAT

I SAMUEL 1:1-20

Has anyone ever made fun of you because of the way you look, because of something you did, or because of something you didn't want to do? It's not fun to be teased. Teasing hurts our feelings. Sometimes, it even makes us want to cry.

Hannah, a woman from our story today, knows how that feels. Hannah was made fun of because she could not have kids. Her husband actually had two wives (the other wife's name was Peninnah). Peninnah had lots of children, but Hannah was not blessed with any children.

GOD'S DAILY SPECIAL

"This went on year after year. Whenever Hannah went up to the house of the Lord, her rival provoked her till she wept and would not eat."
1 Samuel 1:7

Peninnah liked to tease Hannah all the time because she had children and Hannah did not. This made Hannah very sad, and she cried a lot. It even made her so sad that she didn't want anything to eat.

Hannah's husband, Elkanah, loved Hannah and he wanted her to eat, but she was too sad. However, one day they went to the temple and Hannah began praying to God. She cried out to God in her deep sorrow and asked Him to bless her with a son. She even promised God that if He blessed her with a son, she would give him back to God.

It was during her prayer time that the priest, Eli, saw her in the temple. Hannah was acting differently than how most people act when they pray. She was praying out loud, but no sound was coming out of her mouth. Her lips were moving, but nothing could be heard. Eli thought she had been drinking too much wine. But she quickly told him she wasn't drunk, she was just deeply sad because she was not able to have children.

After she told Eli what she was praying for, he said, "Go in peace, and may the God of Israel grant you what you have asked of him" (1 Samuel 1:17). When Hannah left the temple, guess what she did? She ate food! She was finally at peace and wanted something to eat!

God heard Hannah's prayers and blessed her with a son. She called him Samuel, which means "because I asked the Lord for him" (1 Samuel 1:20). When Samuel was old enough, Hannah was true to her word and gave him back to the Lord. Samuel lived in the temple and served God with Eli.

I love Hannah's story because it reminds me that we should never stop praying. It also reminds me that God hears our prayers, and He answers our prayers. Be like Hannah...keep praying and trust in the Lord.

Holy God, thank You for loving me and for listening to my prayer. Remind me of Your peace and help me to know You are with me at all times. In Jesus' name, Amen.

FAITH TO-GO

If you were Hannah, what would be the first thing you would eat after having not eaten for a while?

30

JONATHAN EATS HONEY

I SAMUEL 14:24-30

Picture this: You walk into your house after playing outside all day. As you walk into your kitchen, the smell of freshly baked chocolate chip cookies hits you—and it smells so good! You run straight to the plate of warm cookies and take a handful of them, because they are sitting there, waiting to be eaten. You are so thankful your mom baked some cookies for your family!

A little while later, your mom walks in and notices that several cookies are missing. She questions all of your family members and finally figures out that you are the one who ate the chocolate chip cookies. She is upset because those cookies were not for your family. She was making a specific amount of cookies to deliver to the kids in your brother's class at school. Now she'll have to make more because you ate so many!

> ## GOD'S DAILY SPECIAL
>
> "...So he reached out the end of the staff that was in his hand and dipped it into the honeycomb. He raised his hand to his mouth, and his eyes brightened."
> 1 Samuel 14:27

This is exactly what happened to Jonathan and his dad, Saul. Saul was the King of Israel, and Jonathan was part of his army. In today's story, they were fighting the Philistines. Jonathan and his arms-bearer decided to go out on their own while the Israelite army was resting one night. While they were gone, King Saul made an oath and told his whole army to follow it, too. He said they were fighting well against the Philistines and he didn't want to mess that up. From then on, no one could eat anything until they had completely defeated the Philistines.

On his way back to the camp, Jonathan saw a field full of honey. He scooped up the honey and ate it. It was so good that his eyes brightened with delight. Then, one of the soldiers yelled at him, asking him why he had eaten when his dad, King Saul, had made everyone promise not to eat! Jonathan then realized that he had messed up.

Jonathan was ready to take his punishment for breaking the oath (even though he didn't know about it when he ate the honey), but the other Israelites stood up for him because they liked Jonathan and he had done so much to help them defeat the Philistines. They had forgiven him, and so did God.

Think back to the cookie scenario in the beginning of this devotion. Would your mom have forgiven you for eating the cookies she made for your brother's class? Yes! She might have been upset, but she would definitely have forgiven you. And God forgives us, too. No matter what you have done, God will forgive you. You only need to ask.

Holy God, forgive me for things I have done wrong. Help me to know the difference between right and wrong and to do what You ask me to do. Amen.

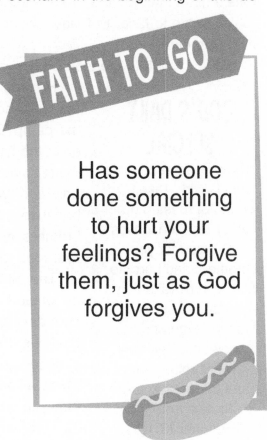

FAITH TO-GO

Has someone done something to hurt your feelings? Forgive them, just as God forgives you.

31

DAVID FEEDS THE TROOPS
I SAMUEL 17:17-58

When you read today's Bible story, something might have sounded familiar. That's because this is the story of David vs. Goliath! You know, the story about the young shepherd boy who defeats a giant that no other man in the Israelite army could even get up the nerve to face. But David wasn't afraid. He faced that giant and killed him!

Did you catch the reason David was there in the first place? He was delivering food to his brothers and the troops! David didn't go to the camp because he heard about the giant the Israelites needed to defeat. He didn't go because he thought he was the only one who could help. He just went because his dad told him to check on his brothers, who were in the army, and deliver food to them.

GOD'S DAILY SPECIAL

"Now Jesse said to his son David, 'Take this ephah of roasted grain and these ten loaves of bread for your brothers and hurry to their camp. Take along these ten cheeses to the commander of their unit. See how your brothers are and bring back some assurance from them.'"
1 Samuel 17:17-18

The Bible says David took an ephah of roasted grain (which was about 36 pounds), ten loaves of bread, and ten cheeses (picture big round blocks of cheese, not grated or sliced cheese). This was a lot of food, especially for one family to take to the troops.

I love what happens next.

When David arrived with the food, he saw the Israelites getting ready to go to battle. I can picture David getting super excited, because he's always loved to be in on the action. After all, he is a shepherd who has to protect his sheep, fighting off lions and bears who try to attack them.

He quickly left the food with the supplies manager and ran to the battle lines to find his brothers. First, he made sure to ask them how they were doing (something his father specifically told him to do). Then Goliath stepped out, and everyone ran away in fear! But not David. He stepped up to the plate with just a slingshot and five smooth stones and gave Israel the victory over the Philistines!

David and Goliath is a great story about conquering our fears and trusting the Lord. It reminds us that there is nothing to fear because God is with us. Today, I hope you learned even more about this story and why David went to the battle. And now you know that it all began with a shepherd delivering food.

Mighty God, thank You for helping me learn something new today about the story of David and Goliath. Thank You for David's family who thought to help feed the troops when they needed it the most. Thank You for feeding me and helping me stay healthy. In Jesus' name, Amen.

FAITH TO-GO

Create a card for someone you know who serves or has served in the military. Draw pictures and write an encouraging note. Let them know Jesus loves them.

32

NO FOOD FOR DAVID

I SAMUEL 25:1-13

Hunger is a big problem in our world. There are many people (some close by and some far away in other countries) who are hungry because of a lack of food. They have no way to buy food and no place to go to eat food.

David and his supporters were hungry while they were on the run from King Saul. They didn't have a place to get food, and they really needed something to eat.

GOD'S DAILY SPECIAL

"Why should I take my bread and water, and the meat I have slaughtered for my shearers, and give it to men coming from who knows where?"

1 Samuel 25:11

David heard about a rich man named Nabal who lived near their camp. He had 1,000 goats and 3,000 sheep (wow!). His wife's name was Abigail, who was very kind. Nabal, on the other hand, was very mean.

While Nabal was in the field shearing sheep, David sent his servants to tell Nabal they had watched over his shepherds and sheep while they were in the field. They protected his animals, so they asked him if he would give them some food in return. They were hungry, and they knew he had enough food to share with them.

But do you think mean Nabal cared about any of that?

Absolutely not!

Nabal laughed at them and said, "Who is this David? Who is this son of Jesse? Many servants are breaking away from their masters these days. Why should I take my bread and water, and the meat I have slaughtered for my shearers, and give it to men coming from who knows where?" (1 Samuel 25:10-11).

Wow. Nabal was a stingy man, wasn't he? He didn't know David and his men, so he didn't owe them anything. He didn't have to feed them any food at all.

Does God ask us to turn our backs on people who are hungry? No, of course not! God actually tells us to feed His people. He tells us to take care of those who are in need. He asks us to give food to the poor.

David was not a happy camper after Nabal told him no. He was so angry that he rallied the troops and was ready to attack Nabal and his family. But one person stopped him, and we will read about her tomorrow.

Loving God, help me see those who are hungry and who need something to eat. Help me to listen to You and to feed those who are in need. Give me the boldness to do as You have asked us to do. Amen.

FAITH TO-GO

Find a food pantry or soup kitchen in your city where you might be able to help. Have your parents call them and find out ways your family can serve those in need.

33

ABIGAIL SAVES THE DAY

I SAMUEL 25:14-44

Superheroes come in all shapes and sizes. That means anyone who does good when there is evil all around can be a superhero. Yesterday, we thought David would be the superhero of this story, but he was not!

The superhero of this story is a woman named Abigail. She was Nabal's wife, the man in yesterday's story who refused to give David and his men any food, even though they had watched over Nabal's shepherds and flocks in the field. All David wanted was some food to eat. But Nabal wouldn't give in.

> ## GOD'S DAILY SPECIAL
>
> "And let this gift, which your servant has brought to my lord, be given to the men who follow you."
> 1 Samuel 25:27

One of Nabal's servants told Abigail what had happened. He also told her that David and his men were getting ready to attack them because of Nabal. None of the servants wanted this, and he urged Abigail to do something.

So what was Abigail's solution?

Food! She brought a lot of food to David and his men. Here's a list of what she brought: two hundred loaves of bread, two skins of wine, five dressed sheep, five seahs of roasted grain (which is about sixty pounds), a hundred cakes of raisins, and two hundred cakes of pressed figs (1 Samuel 25:18). She did not spare anything. She brought David and his men all the food they needed so they would not attack Nabal and his land. The men were very grateful.

Do you want to know why I think David was so upset?

Because he was hangry!

Have you ever heard that term before? He was hungry and he was angry—he was hangry. I don't know about you, but sometimes I get hangry when I haven't eaten anything for a while. I get grouchy when I just need something to eat! After I've had a snack or a meal, I am usually a happier person to be around.

David was probably hangry that day. He hadn't eaten in a while, and he was doing everything he could to find food for himself and his men. When Nabal refused to give them any food, his hunger turned into anger!

I love the way God used Abigail to save the day! He gave her the idea to bring David and his men food to satisfy their hunger and help them feel at peace. Her kindness (and the food) calmed David down and stopped him from doing something he would regret. Abigail was a superhero that day. And food was her superpower! Thank You, God, for food!

Almighty God, thank You for Abigail and her ability to show kindness to David. Thank You for the food given to them to help them. Please help me show kindness to someone just like Abigail did to David. Amen.

FAITH TO-GO

Write down some ways you can use food to show kindness to someone.

34

DAVID AND HIS ARMY FUEL UP

I CHRONICLES 12:23-40

Have you ever heard the expression, "It looks like you're going to feed an army!" That's another way of saying, "You sure do have a lot of food to eat!"

That expression would have been very true on the day David and his army were gearing up for battle.

To give you a little background: King Saul had recently died, and the majority of Israel agreed that David would become the next king (a decision God had already blessed). But when you are a king, you must have an army of people who can fight for you and your country. Israel wanted David to be king, so they gathered men from each of the twelve tribes of Israel to be in his army. If you added up all the army members listed from each tribe (found in 1 Chronicles 12:24-37), you would find a total of 340,822. That is a lot of men!

To prepare for battle, they needed to fuel up—which means they needed to eat! For three days, David and all of his men ate. The Bible says there were "plentiful supplies of flour, fig cakes, raisin cakes, wine, olive oil, cattle and sheep" (1 Chronicles 12:40).

Who supplied all of this food for the men? The Bible says the soldiers' families provided the food they needed to eat to prepare for battle. It also says their neighbors sent food via donkeys, camels, mules, and oxen. Can you imagine being in your home, looking out the window, and seeing all these animals walking down the road carrying food? That would certainly have been a sight to see!

To live, we need food. To prepare for difficult and strenuous activities, we need food. Have you ever tried to run a race without eating something beforehand? If you have, you might have felt lightheaded, dizzy, or sick to your stomach. You might not even have made it to the finish line because you didn't feel well.

It's important to eat well before we exercise or do strenuous activities. It fuels our bodies. God knew David and his army would need food before they could take on the challenges they would face in the days ahead. God provided what they needed, and He provides for us every day, too.

Jehovah-Jireh, thank You for being my Provider. Help me to open my eyes to see all the ways You provide for me. In Jesus' name, Amen.

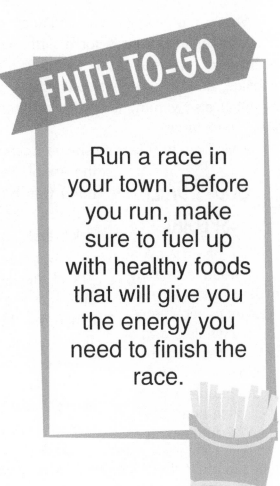

FAITH TO-GO

Run a race in your town. Before you run, make sure to fuel up with healthy foods that will give you the energy you need to finish the race.

35

A PARTY IN JERUSALEM

2 SAMUEL 6:17-19

What's one thing you can find at almost any party? Food!

Whether the party is for a birthday, graduation, wedding, or holiday, you will most likely find food there from cake, ice cream, cookies, hamburgers, hot dogs, chips, pizza, steak, to just about anything else yummy that you can think of. We like to celebrate things with food!

David liked to celebrate special occasions, too, and the day that the Ark of the Lord (or Ark of the Covenant) was brought into Jerusalem was a day for the entire nation of Israel to celebrate!

> ## GOD'S DAILY SPECIAL
>
> "Then he gave a loaf of bread, a cake of dates and a cake of raisins to each person in the whole crowd of Israelites, both men and women. And all the people went to their homes."
> 2 Samuel 6:19

You might be asking, "What is the Ark of the Lord?" The Ark was a box, and this box was very special. It contained the tablets Moses engraved the Ten Commandments on. It was also holy because it represented the presence of God. It was so holy that no one was allowed to touch it, so it had to be carried using poles or carts.

David had already tried a couple of times to move the Ark of the Lord to Jerusalem and had failed, but on this day, he was finally successful! David and the people celebrated with dancing, sounds of trumpets, and lots of shouts. It was an exciting day in Israel!

After the Ark of the Lord was placed inside a special tent, David made sacrifices and offerings to God. Then, he decided that everyone in Jerusalem needed to celebrate with food! He gave every person a loaf of bread, a cake of dates, and a cake of raisins. This might not be the kind of food you would serve at a party today, but back then, it was considered a feast.

What are some things we celebrate as Christians? We celebrate the birth of Jesus (Christmas), the day Jesus rose from the dead (Easter), the day the Holy Spirit came to this earth (Pentecost), and even the day we are saved and the day we get baptized. At most of these celebrations, we like to serve food! As we eat, we give thanks to God for all He has done for us. We thank God for who He is and how He has blessed us. So today, go out and celebrate! Throw a party and thank God for His love for you. That's a celebration worth having every day!

Loving God, today I celebrate You! I am so thankful for the many ways You love me. Help me to always remember Your love and Your faithfulness. In Jesus' name, Amen.

FAITH TO-GO

Throw a party today for God with your family. Serve some food and thank God for how He has blessed your family.

FOOD TRUCK EQUIPMENT

In order to have a food truck ministry, you will need some equipment! You need appliances to cook and store your food, and items to use to prepare your food.

In the space below, write down some pieces of equipment you will need to use for your specific food truck.

FOOD TRUCK EQUIPMENT

IN THE BOX BELOW, DRAW A PICTURE OF THE INSIDE OF YOUR FOOD TRUCK.
WHERE WILL EVERYTHING GO?

36

ZIBA GIVES DAVID FOOD

2 SAMUEL 16:1-4

Have you ever received food you were not expecting? Maybe a friend gave you a treat at school or a family friend brought a meal to your house one night. I bet that unexpected food was a nice surprise for you!

King David received a gift of food one day that was probably unexpected. Ziba, a friend of Mephibosheth (who was the son of David's best friend, Jonathan, and King Saul's grandson), met David and delivered him lots of food. In fact, he brought a whole row of donkeys loaded down with food! They were strapped with two hundred loaves of bread, a hundred cakes of raisins, a hundred cakes of figs, and a skin of wine. Can you imagine being greeted at your house with this much food? You might be quite surprised if this much food showed up at your house. You might even ask why someone gave you so much food.

That's exactly what David did. In 2 Samuel 16:2, he immediately asked Ziba, "Why have you brought these?" Ziba gives a direct answer, too: "The donkeys are for the king's household to ride on, the bread and fruit are for the men to eat, and the wine is to refresh those who become exhausted in the wilderness." What a specific answer!

GOD'S DAILY SPECIAL

"Then the king asked Ziba, 'Why have you brought these?' Ziba answered, 'The donkeys are for the king's household to ride on, the bread and fruit are for the men to eat, and the wine is to refresh those who become exhausted in the wilderness.'"
2 Samuel 16:2

Ziba was very thoughtful and kind to bring all this food to David for his men. He knew David and his men needed the food and the donkeys. Why? Because King David was on the run from his son, Absalom, who was trying to kill him so he could become king instead! It was a crazy time for David. He left Jerusalem in a hurry, and he probably wasn't able to pack as much as he would have liked, especially in the food department. Ziba knew where David was going to be, so he delivered the food and donkeys the king would need.

Maybe you know someone who is going through a hard time or you have a friend who could use a little bit of extra love because they are sad. Talk to your parents about what you could do for them. Maybe you could bring a meal to their house or pack some extra food in your lunchbox to share with them. Bringing food to friends and family who are in need is a very generous and kind thing to do. It shows them how much you love and care about them. You are sharing God's love when you share food!

Most Holy God, help me to be kind and generous to those in need. Show me someone who could use a meal to brighten their day. Help me to love others the way You love me. In Jesus' name, Amen.

FAITH TO-GO

Do you know someone who has recently had a baby born into their family, or had surgery, or has lost a loved one? Bring a meal to them and show them you care about them.

37

SOLOMON'S DAILY PROVISIONS

I KINGS 4:20-28

Who provides the food you need every day? Your answer is probably whoever you live with, whether that's your parents, grandparents, aunts, uncles, or foster parents. They provide food for you because they love you and want you to live a healthy life.

The people of Israel were great in number. The Bible says they were "as numerous as the sand on the seashore" (1 Kings 4:20). Think about how big that number is! There is so much sand on the seashore that we couldn't even count it all!

GOD'S DAILY SPECIAL

"The people of Judah and Israel were as numerous as the sand on the seashore; they ate, they drank and they were happy."
1 Kings 4:20

Just like your family provides for you, there was a king in Israel who provided daily food for his people. He was the wisest king Israel had ever had. His name was Solomon, and he was the son of King David. After David passed away, Solomon became king. God asked Solomon what he wanted, and Solomon asked for wisdom. And God blessed him with great wisdom.

Along with the blessing of wisdom came the blessing of food and other resources the kingdom of Israel needed. Solomon used these blessings for the whole nation of Israel, and he provided food for the people daily. The Bible says that every day Solomon provided "thirty cors of the finest flour and sixty cors of meal, ten head of stall-fed cattle, twenty of pasture-fed cattle and a hundred sheep and goats, as well as deer, gazelles, roebucks, and choice fowl" (1 Kings 4:22-23). You might be wondering how much a "cor" is. A cor is equal to 5 ½ tons. So thirty cors of flour and sixty cors of meal is equal to tons and tons of flour and meal! Plus, he provided lots of animals for the people to eat. It's safe to say the people of Israel were well-fed!

Solomon was not only a wise king, but a generous and obedient king, too. He followed the Lord and used the gifts God had given him. He used the wisdom God gave to help those in his kingdom. He used the food God gave to provide enough for every person in the kingdom of Israel.

What blessings has the Lord given you? Are you using those blessings to serve others? Think about what those blessings are, then brainstorm ways you can use them to bless the people around you.

Most Holy God, thank You for blessing my family. Help me to always see the blessings You give us and help me to use those blessings to bless someone else. Amen.

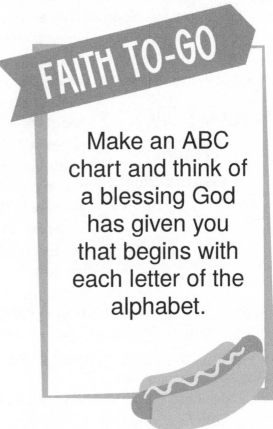

FAITH TO-GO

Make an ABC chart and think of a blessing God has given you that begins with each letter of the alphabet.

38

RAVENS FEED ELIJAH

I KINGS 17:1-6

Have you ever seen the movie *Snow White*? It's an old Disney movie, but it's one of my favorites. Snow White lives in the woods, and she is loved by all the creatures who live there, including the seven dwarfs, the birds, and all the animals. I remember watching birds help her clean the house and fold the clothes. The birds helped Snow White whenever she needed it.

There's a story in the Bible about birds helping a man when he needed it, too! His name was Elijah, and he was a prophet (which means he got messages from God about the future and shared those messages with the people). Elijah told King Ahab that God said there would be no rain in the land of Israel for the next few years until God commanded it.

> ### GOD'S DAILY SPECIAL
>
> "You will drink from the brook, and I have directed the ravens to supply you with food there."
> 1 Kings 17:4

Ahab, who was an evil king, did not like Elijah telling him things like this. Elijah was afraid of what Ahab might do to him, so God told Elijah to go away. Specifically, He told him to hide in the Kerith Ravine and drink from the brook there. God instructed ravens to supply Elijah with food. Imagine what might have been going through Elijah's mind when God told him all of this...

Okay, Lord, I'll go hide. Thank You for giving me a safe shelter away from King Ahab. He is a scary king. Thank You for providing water for me to drink because I know I'll get super thirsty. But I'm a little confused about how ravens will bring me food to eat? How will they know where I am? How will they know what to bring me? But I trust You, Lord, and I can't wait to see how ravens bring me food.

No matter what Elijah was thinking, he went to the Kerith Ravine, trusting the Lord to provide for him. And guess what? The ravens did show up to bring him food! Every morning and every evening, they flew in with bread and meat. I'm sure it was cool to see birds bringing him food. But what's even cooler is knowing that what God had promised actually happened! I would be so grateful, and I know Elijah was, too.

Do you need to trust God with something? Whatever it is, pray about it. Then, believe God will provide for you and will be with you. It might take a short time or a long time, but God hears your prayers and blesses those who trust in Him.

Father God, help me to trust You just like Elijah trusted You to provide food for him with the ravens. I believe in You, Lord, and I want to honor You at all times. Amen.

FAITH TO-GO

Feed God's birds today! Buy some birdseed from the store, along with a birdfeeder. Hang it in a tree in your yard and fill it with food. Then watch as the birds come and eat. Thank God for the blessing of the birds.

39

ELIJAH AND THE WIDOW AT ZAREPHATH

I KINGS 17:7-24

Has your family ever moved? What were a few of the things your parents did to prepare to move to another city?

I would guess they looked for houses to buy or rent, visited the area to see where you could eat and shop, and even checked out the schools you would be attending. They made sure you would have all you'd need in your new city.

GOD'S DAILY SPECIAL

"Go at once to Zarephath in the region of Sidon and stay there. I have directed a widow there to supply you with food."
1 Kings 17:9

In today's story, Elijah is on the move again. And guess what? God will once again provide food for him in this new place. This time, God tells him to go to the town of Zarephath. In this town, God provided a widow (a woman whose husband has died) to give him food.

Elijah met a woman at the town gate and asked her for water and a piece of bread. She was a little hesitant at first, because she knew she barely had enough flour and olive oil left in her house to feed herself and her son. If she couldn't feed herself and her son, how could she try to feed a stranger, too?

But Elijah knew God would provide for all of them. How do you think he knew this? Remember, he had just been fed by ravens for a while. I believe he knew that if God provided ravens to feed him, God would provide enough food to feed himself, the widow, and her son.

And God did provide! God said, "The jar of flour will not be used up and the jug of oil will not run dry until the day the Lord sends rain on the land" (1 Kings 17:14). That nearly-empty jar of flour and olive oil became a jar that never went dry. It was always filled with enough flour and olive oil to feed the three of them.

Can you imagine the excitement and amazement on the faces of the widow and her son? Here was a man, who showed up in their town, asked her (a poor widow) for food to eat, and who promised God would provide enough food for all of them. I might have initially felt a little uncertain, too, like they did, but I am thankful she listened and obeyed what God told Elijah. She had such great faith to believe that God would provide!

God is so good! He provides all our needs and will always be with us. Praise be to God!

Father God, thank You for providing the food I need. Please provide food to all those who do not have enough. Amen.

FAITH TO-GO

Make bread today and donate it to your local soup kitchen or food pantry.

40

AN ANGEL PROVIDES FOOD FOR ELIJAH

I KINGS 19:1-9

What do you like to do on a long road trip? To keep yourself from getting bored, maybe you listen to music, play video games, talk to your siblings and parents, or play fun road trip games in the car with your family.

When I travel, I love to sleep! My parents told me that any time we had to travel a long way when I was a kid, they would check the rearview mirror to find me sleeping. I especially loved when they woke me up from my car nap and said, "It's time to eat," because that meant we were stopping at a fast food restaurant for a meal. I always loved eating out as a kid!

GOD'S DAILY SPECIAL

"Then he lay down under the bush and fell asleep. All at once an angel touched him and said, 'Get up and eat.'"

1 Kings 19:5

In today's story about Elijah, we find him traveling (actually, he's running for his life because Queen Jezebel wants to kill him). He's been traveling for a long time, and he's so tired of it that he's in tears, crying out to God. When he couldn't walk any further, he took a nap! A little later, he was woken up by an angel that said, "Get up and eat" (1 Kings 19:5). I'm sure Elijah must have been a little disoriented and unsure of where he was. But when he looked around, he found food! Near his head, he found some bread that had been baked over hot coals and a jar of water.

That bread and water must have hit the spot because he decided to go back to sleep again! But the same angel came back later to wake him up. Again, this angel brought bread and water. This time, the angel told Elijah that he needed to get up and eat, because the journey would be too much for him if he didn't have the food he needed.

After the angel delivered two meals to Elijah, he had the strength to travel forty days and forty nights. That's a long time! God provided the food Elijah would need to make the long journey to Mount Horeb, which actually ends up being the place he sees God! (See 1 Kings 19:10-18.)

Remember that God's food helps to keep us going so we can continue to do His work in this world. Don't skip a meal. Fuel up so you can do all you can for God in this world.

Holy God, help me to do all I can to follow You. Give me the food I need to bring me strength and energy to do that. In Jesus' name, Amen.

FAITH TO-GO

On your next road trip, make a stop at a fast food restaurant. Buy an extra meal or a gift card and give away to someone who might be in need.

41

THE WIDOW'S OIL

2 KINGS 4:1-7

Raise your hand if you have to pay bills! I am fairly certain that you aren't raising your hand, because you're a kid! You don't pay bills because you don't have a job. Your parents are the ones who pay the bills and make sure your family has what they need.

Can I share a cool story with you? Once, I received a bill in the mail that was unexpected and not in our budget. My husband and I wondered how we were going to pay this bill. But one day, I went to work and found an envelope in my mailbox. When I opened it, there was enough cash inside to cover the unexpected bill. We hadn't told anyone about this bill, so no one knew how much it cost. The money just showed up. I knew it was from God!

A similar situation happened in our Bible story today. A widow did not have enough money to pay off the debt she owed. If she didn't pay her debts, she would lose her sons. She was very sad and didn't know what to do.

> ## GOD'S DAILY SPECIAL
>
> "Elisha replied to her, 'How can I help you? Tell me, what do you have in your house?' 'Your servant has nothing there at all,' she said, 'except a small jar of olive oil.'"
> 2 Kings 4:2

So she went to the prophet Elisha for help, and he told her to do something that might seem a little strange to you. He asked her what she had in her house. She told him she had nothing except a jar of oil. How could a jar of oil help her get out of debt?

Elisha told her to find as many jars as she could, and to use the oil she had to fill them all up. She was even supposed to ask friends and family members for more empty jars to use.

Imagine this request from the widow's viewpoint. She probably thought Elisha was a little crazy, because there was no way she had enough oil in her house to fill a lot of empty jars. Her only jar wasn't even full!

She might have questioned how oil was going to help her, but she obeyed, doing exactly what Elisha told her. She was able to fill all the empty jars to the top with oil! As soon as she finished filling the last jar, the oil stopped flowing. Amazing, right? Then, Elisha told her to sell the jars. When she did, she had enough money to pay off all her debts.

I love this story because it reminds me that God can use simple things (like oil) to provide what we need. Never doubt God's amazing power and His creative ways of providing for you.

Lord of All, thank You for providing for my family. Help my parents and myself to trust in You to provide all we need, even in times when it seems like there is no hope. I love You, Lord. Amen.

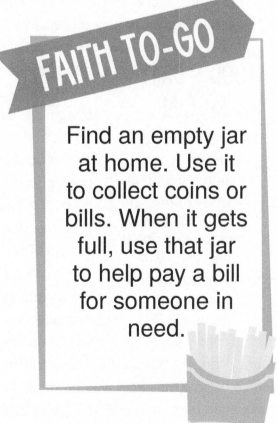

FAITH TO-GO

Find an empty jar at home. Use it to collect coins or bills. When it gets full, use that jar to help pay a bill for someone in need.

42

FEEDING OF 100 MEN

2 KINGS 4:42-44

You might already know about the time Jesus fed 5,000 people in the New Testament (see John 6:1-15). If you do know that story, this story in 2 Kings, when Elisha feeds 100 men, might seem like no big deal. Jesus fed more than that.

To me, this story is just as amazing as the New Testament story, because this story was a precursor to the miracle Jesus would perform. Both stories show just how capable and amazing our God is.

In today's verses, we find a man bringing Elisha twenty loaves of barley bread and some heads of new grain. He was probably excited to give it to him, hoping that Elisha could use it to serve a small group of people, like his friends or some other prophets.

But Elisha asked this man to do something with the twenty loaves of bread and new heads of grain that he probably never expected. Elisha told the man to serve the food to one hundred men. I can just picture the look on the man's face when Elisha told him to do this! His brow was probably furrowed. His forehead might have even been wrinkled. His look of confusion was probably priceless. He knew there was no way that twenty loaves of bread and

GOD'S DAILY SPECIAL

"A man came from Baal Shalishah, bringing the man of God twenty loaves of barley bread baked from the first ripe grain, along with some heads of new grain."
2 Kings 4:42

new heads of grain would feed one hundred men. There just wasn't enough to go around.

But Elisha was insistent. He even told the man there would be leftovers! Still, the man was probably confused. But he obeyed what Elisha had said, because he trusted the Lord and he trusted that Elisha was a servant of the Lord. If Elisha said that God would provide enough food, then he would follow what Elisha told him to do.

You already know what happens next: the one hundred men ate the bread and grain and had some left over! Isn't that amazing? When we believe in God and trust in His power, we can be confident that God will provide, even if it seems impossible.

Almighty God, You are so awesome! Thank You for the many ways You provide for me. Help me to trust You, even in situations that seem impossible. Amen.

FAITH TO-GO

Search through your pantry and find food that you can donate to your local food pantry.

RECIPE OF A MENU ITEM

Every food truck owner probably has a few recipes written down. These may be family recipes or recipes they have made from scratch.

Pick one of your menu items. In the space below, write down all the ingredients needed to make it.

On the next page, create a recipe card for this item. Take the ingredients you wrote above, and write them down, along with instructions of how to make this food item.

FOOD TRUCK RECIPE

INGREDIENTS

_____
_____
_____

DIRECTIONS

_____
_____
_____
_____
_____

43

CELEBRATING THE UNDERSTANDING OF THE LAW

NEHEMIAH 8:1-12

Have you ever read the Bible, understood what it said, then celebrated your understanding with a party and some food?

Maybe you haven't, but I can't think of a better way to celebrate the understanding of the Word of God! That's exactly what the Israelites did in Nehemiah 8. The Israelites had been exiled (forced to move out) from Israel and taken to live in Babylon. They were captured by the Babylonians because they had disobeyed the Lord. During their exile, the land of Israel was nearly destroyed.

> ## GOD'S DAILY SPECIAL
>
> "Then all the people went away to eat and drink, to send portions of food and to celebrate with great joy, because they now understood the words that had been made known to them."
>
> Nehemiah 8:12

After seventy long years in Babylon, the Israelites were finally allowed to return to their land. Ezra (the priest) and Nehemiah (the governor) had come back to Israel beforehand to rebuild the temple and the wall around Jerusalem. These two men of God played a special role in restoring the land of Israel.

About seven months after they had settled back into their towns in Israel, they all came to hear the reading of the Book of the Law (which we now know as the Pentateuch, which are the first five books of the Old Testament). Ezra read the law to them and the Israelites rejoiced, cried, grieved, and were filled with joy. Lots of emotions! You see, before they were exiled, they spoke Hebrew. But when they moved to Babylon, they had to learn to speak Aramaic[3]. They were there for seventy years, and after such a long time, they had probably forgotten a lot of the Hebrew language.

But Ezra, Nehemiah, and the Levite priests helped them understand God's Law and how to obey it. The Israelites were filled with so much joy that they wanted to celebrate! They went back to their homes and ate, drank, and had a party! They were so excited to be able to understand God's Law clearly again. They loved the Lord and wanted to follow and obey His commands. That's a great reason to celebrate!

Powerful God, help me to understand Your Word. May I always find joy and comfort when I read it. Remind me to celebrate when I understand. Amen.

---

3   https://www.britannica.com/topic/Aramaic-language

FAITH TO-GO

Plan a Scripture Reading Party with your family. Pick a passage from the Bible to read together. Make sure everyone understands it. Afterwards, celebrate your understanding with a party! Serve your favorite foods and drinks.

44

ESTHER FASTS

ESTHER 4

Have you ever heard the term "fasting?"

I'm not talking about doing something fast. When someone says they are fasting, it means they are going without food for a period of time. Sometimes your doctor might ask you not to eat for a certain amount of time before a test or surgery. But most of the time, this term refers to a person who is fasting from food for spiritual reasons. Fasting and prayer go hand in hand. Usually, when people fast, they also are praying for something specific.

GOD'S DAILY SPECIAL

"Go, gather together all the Jews who are in Susa, and fast for me. Do not eat or drink for three days, night or day. I and my attendants will fast as you do."
Esther 4:16

That's exactly what Queen Esther asked all the Jewish people to do for three days.

Esther's cousin, Mordecai, had heard some disturbing news from Haman, one of the servants of King Xerxes. Haman wanted to kill all the Jews. He did not like them, so he made plans for the king to sign a decree (a law) saying he could kill all the Jews. Mordecai was upset because he was Jewish, and so was Queen Esther. He needed Esther to find a way to stop Haman.

Queen Esther did the only thing she could do. She fasted and prayed, and she asked everyone else to do it with her. She asked all the Jewish people to go without food for three days, and to spend those days praying that God would save the Jewish people. They needed to focus all their time and all their prayers on asking God to help them.

People still practice fasting today. Some people may fast for three days, and others may fast for a meal or two. Some people choose to fast from something that keeps them distracted from God (like TV, social media, or video games). Fasting can be done in many different ways, but its purpose is always to draw closer to the Lord.

Is there something you need to pray about? Maybe you could fast. For kids, I would not recommend a three-day fast from food or drink like Esther did. Instead, you could fast from eating a particular food for three days (but not something that you already don't like). Maybe you could stop watching your favorite tv show for three days and instead, pray about the thing you need God's help with. Think about it. How could you fast?

Holy God, help me to hear You. Help me to listen and obey You. Help me to focus my time on You. Amen.

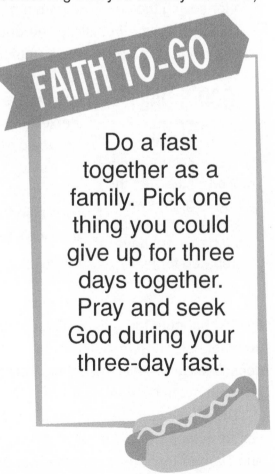

FAITH TO-GO

Do a fast together as a family. Pick one thing you could give up for three days together. Pray and seek God during your three-day fast.

45

ESTHER'S BANQUET FOR KING XERXES

ESTHER 5-8

Remember Queen Esther's story yesterday...when we learned about fasting and praying?

God heard Esther's prayers and the Jews were saved! God's plan for saving the Jews involved a banquet with lots of food!

During this time in history, the queen could not go to the king without being summoned. But Esther took a leap of faith and asked to see the king (without him asking to see her first). She was scared, but King Xerxes was pleased to see her and said he would grant her any request.

Esther asked the king to come to a banquet she had prepared for him. She also asked him to bring Haman, the king's servant who wanted to kill the Jews.

> ### GOD'S DAILY SPECIAL
>
> "'If it pleases the king,' replied Esther, 'let the king, together with Haman, come today to a banquet I have prepared for him.'"
>
> Esther 5:4

They had a big feast! Can you imagine what kinds of food were served at this big banquet for a king? There could have been steak, lobster, gourmet hamburgers, salads, rolls, and lots of desserts! The Bible doesn't tell us what kinds of food Esther chose, but it's fun to imagine what might have been served.

The king loved the banquet so much that he was ready to say yes to Esther, no matter what she asked. But Esther wanted him and Haman to come to another banquet the next day. Then, she promised to tell the king her request.

So the king doesn't just get one feast, he gets two! I wonder if they served the same thing both days or if they served two totally different menus? We don't know that, but we do know that Esther used food to influence the king's decision to grant her request. I think she knew he loved food so much that if she fed him his favorite foods, he might give her the one thing she wanted. (Remember, she wanted to save the lives of her people, the Jews.)

The story does end with the Jews being saved (Haman was the one who was killed in the end). Now God's people could live peacefully, thanks to Esther's fast, prayers, and banquets of food!

Incredible God, thank You for the story of Esther and how You used her to help save the Jews. Help me to listen to You just as Esther listened to You. In Jesus' name, Amen.

FAITH TO-GO

Plan a banquet of food one night for your family. Make a list of all your family's favorite foods and serve them. During the banquet, make sure to pray and thank God for the many blessings He has given you.

46

ARE YOU THIRSTY?

PSALM 42:1-4

No matter where I go, I always carry one thing with me. Can you guess what it is?

A water bottle.

I cannot stand to be thirsty without having any water nearby. I have a bottle of water in my car, in my office, beside my chair in the living room, on my nightstand in case I wake up thirsty, and even when I walk around my neighborhood for exercise. A bottle of water is never far from me!

> ### GOD'S DAILY SPECIAL
>
> "As the deer pants for streams of water, so my soul pants for you, my God."
> Psalm 42:1

The psalmist (that's someone who writes Psalms) was thirsty, too—but not the kind of thirsty you may think of when you want something to drink. He was thirsty for God, which means he longed to be close to God. He wanted to feel God's presence and worship God with all his heart. He was thirsty for everything about God!

Let's think about something for a minute. What things do you need to live? We would all start our lists with air, food and water, right? The psalmist actually writes about those things in the first four verses of this chapter: a deer panting (air) for water, and tears serving as his food (which means he was sad and didn't eat anything). Have you ever put God on the list of what you need to live? Maybe you've never thought about that. But God is definitely needed. We need Him to save us so we can live forever with Him in heaven.

My hope is that you will thirst for God like this psalmist did. I pray you will always have a strong desire to be close to the Lord. I pray you will do everything you can to learn more about Him. I pray you will spend time in prayer every day. I pray you will worship Him daily (just listen to some of your favorite praise and worship songs). I pray you will love the Lord with all your heart. And if you don't know Jesus yet, my prayer is that you will accept Him as your Savior so you can live forever with Him one day.

Be thirsty for God! Get to know Him and walk closely with Him.

Almighty God, I want to know You more. Help me to spend time with You every day so I can be close to You. Amen.

FAITH TO-GO

Carry a bottle of water with you today. When you take a drink, remember to thirst for God (and then go spend time with Him).

47

FOOD FOR ALL CREATION

PSALM 104:10-21

Have you ever stopped to think about how all of creation gets its food? God designed food for every living thing on this earth.

Did you know God made water? Now, you and I get water out of the kitchen sink, from a well, or even out of a bottle from the store. But in today's Bible passage, verse 10 tells us the waters flow between the mountains and provide water for all the animals. As I am writing this, I'm sitting beside a river on our annual family camping trip. Over the course of the week, I have watched birds, butterflies, and of course, my dog, Henry, drink from this river. And I know many other animals have come to the edge of the water to quench their thirst while I was sleeping. Water is necessary for all creatures to live!

> ## GOD'S DAILY SPECIAL
>
> "He makes grass grow for the cattle, and plants for people to cultivate – bringing forth food from the earth."
> Psalm 104:14

The psalm also reminds us that God provides grass for the cattle to eat. How many times have you driven by a field and seen cattle grazing? We don't eat grass, but grass is a necessary source of food for cows and lots of other animals.

Next, the psalm tells us that God created plants for people to grow and eat. Raise your hand if your family has a garden that grows things for you to eat! I wish I could raise my hand, but we have deer around our house, and they like to eat anything we plant (which is good for them, but not so good for us). I love that the psalmist tells us that plants were made for us to grow! They were made to feed not only us, but others on the earth.

Finally, the psalmist writes that "the trees of the Lord are well watered" (Psalm 104:16). Maybe you don't think about how trees get their food, but they need water to stay alive, too. Their roots must be fully nourished with water in order to stay strong. If you have seen fallen trees, it could be because they haven't had enough water to feed their roots. When the roots aren't nourished, the trees lose their strength and fall to the ground.

Food is vital for all living things on the earth. I think it's pretty amazing that God didn't create the same foods for all of us. We don't eat grass like cows, and cows don't eat the same foods we eat. We are all different, yet God created food and water so all of us could live on this earth. God is so amazing!

Creator God, thank You for creating food for all of Your creatures on this earth. Help me to remember to thank You before I eat at meal times. I am so thankful for You, Lord. Amen.

FAITH TO-GO

Plant a small garden in your yard or plant some things in 5-gallon buckets (like tomatoes or cucumbers). Share the bounty of your garden with others.

48

FOOD AT THE PROPER TIME

PSALM 145:14-16

How many meals do we typically eat in a day?

If you said three, then you would be correct! We eat three meals a day: breakfast, lunch, and supper. But how many of us actually eat three meals a day? Sometimes we skip a meal because we aren't hungry, or we get so busy we forget to eat. That's not good for our bodies. Maybe you're the opposite and you eat more than three meals a day! That's not good for our bodies, either.

> ### GOD'S DAILY SPECIAL
>
> "The eyes of all look to you, and you give them their food at the proper time."
> Psalm 145:15

Psalm 145:15 says, "The eyes of all look to you, and you give them their food at the proper time." I love that God gives us food at the proper time. The key word here is "proper," which means right. There is a time for us to eat, and a time for us to wait.

I'm going to guess that most of you who skip a meal choose breakfast. You may not be a morning person. You may roll out of the bed, get dressed, and go off to school. You might not even be hungry before you leave for school. But did you know that breakfast is THE most important meal of the day? The food we eat in the morning gives us the energy we need for the day ahead. It wakes up our brains and helps us think. It is good for us to eat breakfast in the morning!

Some of you may skip lunch instead. Maybe you aren't hungry because you had a big breakfast. Maybe you don't like the food in your lunchbox or what's being served in the lunchroom. But it's not good to skip lunch, either. You need food to help keep you going.

Finally, there's supper (or dinner). Sometimes we don't eat because we're busy with extracurricular activities like football, dance, or soccer. Maybe you get so busy doing homework that you don't show up for supper. Maybe you just aren't hungry. Guess what I'm going to say next? That's right: it's not good to skip this meal, either! You need food to sustain your body as you sleep and help you get a good night's rest.

For humans, it's important to eat three meals. If we skip a meal, we aren't feeding our bodies what they need. We aren't letting God feed us at the proper times. God knows when we need food, and that's three times a day. So remember to eat! God has given you the food you need to have a great day!

Giving God, thank You for creating food. Help me to remember to eat three meals a day and to eat healthy foods that will help my body. Amen.

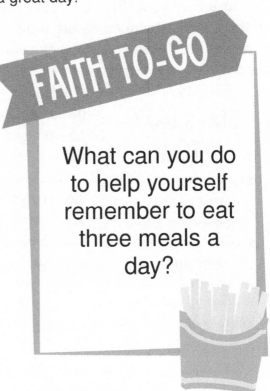

FAITH TO-GO

What can you do to help yourself remember to eat three meals a day?

49

PRAISE THE LORD FOR FOOD

PSALM 145:21

Why do we say a blessing before we eat a meal?

Have you ever thought about that before? Why is it important to thank God for the food we are about to eat?

I love Psalm 145:21, which says, "My mouth will speak in praise of the Lord. Let every creature praise his holy name for ever and ever." You and I are some of those creatures. God created us, and we are His magnificent creations. We are made to praise God and thank Him for the many blessings He gives us. One of those blessings is food, so we should thank Him for the food we eat.

Let's talk about the different blessings we say before meals. Someone in your family might say a prayer, asking God to bless the food. Your family might also say (or sing) one of these blessings:

> ### GOD'S DAILY SPECIAL
>
> "My mouth will speak in praise of the Lord. Let every creature praise his holy name for ever and ever."
> Psalm 145:21

God is great, God is good, let us thank Him for our food. By His hands, we are fed. Give us, Lord, our daily bread. Amen.

God our Father (God our Father), once again (once again), we will ask Your blessing (we will ask Your blessing), Amen (Amen).

For the Lord is good to me, and so I thank the Lord. For giving me the things I need: the sun, and the rain, and the appleseed. The Lord is good to me. Amen. (Johnny Appleseed Blessing)

Thank You, God, for giving us food, thank You, God, for giving us friends. For the friends we meet, for the food we eat. Thank You, God. Amen. (Superman Blessing)

No matter what type of blessing you say before meals, it's important to praise God with our mouths. We may sing a blessing (like one of the ones above), or we may speak a blessing. But no matter which one we choose, we are praising God for the food He has given us to eat.

Blessings can be said at the table with your family, at the lunch table with friends at school, at restaurants when you go out to eat, or even by yourself. Remember to praise God before you eat!

Thank You, God, for giving me food to eat. May my mouth always speak praises to You (even for the foods I don't like to eat). I love You, Lord. Amen.

FAITH TO-GO

Ask your friends at the lunch table if they would like to say a blessing with you before you eat your lunch at school.

FOOD TRUCK GROCERY LIST

It's time to stock your food truck with food!

Every food truck will need to have all the necessary ingredients for everything on your menu. You can't use the truck without having all the food you need to serve!

Look back at all the items on your menu. On the next page, make a grocery list. Write down every ingredient you will need for all the items on your menu. Don't forget anything!

FOOD TRUCK
GROCERY LIST

50

SWEET LIKE A HONEYCOMB

PROVERBS 16:24

Sticks and stones may break my bones, but words will never hurt me.

I learned that saying as a kid. I probably said it when my sister called me a name I didn't like or when someone made fun of me. Saying those words didn't seem to make my sadness or my hurt feelings go away, though. The truth is...words do hurt! Our words are powerful. We have the power to build someone up or break someone down just by the words that come out of our mouth.

> ## GOD'S DAILY SPECIAL
>
> "Gracious words are a honeycomb, sweet to the soul and healing to the bones."
> Proverbs 16:24

King Solomon knew that all too well. I believe that's why he wrote what he did in Proverbs 16:24: "Gracious words are a honeycomb, sweet to the soul and healing to the bones." This wisdom from King Solomon is so true.

Have you ever tasted honey? It is so sweet! But I've never tasted it right off the honeycomb. I hear the honeycomb provides the sweetest form of honey. If you love honey, maybe you'll have a chance to try it off the honeycomb one day.

So, what are gracious words, and how do they relate to the honeycomb?

Using gracious words means being kind when you speak to someone. Solomon compares gracious words to a honeycomb because people in his day ate a lot of honey. He knew they would understand the comparison of gracious words to the sweetness of a honeycomb. We should be kind, caring, and courteous to others all the time. We know how we feel when someone speaks kind words to us. It's sweet, right? We should do the same to others. We want our words to be sweet to them, too. We want our words to be healing, which makes others feel good. We don't want our words to be hurtful, which makes others feel bad.

Speak gracious words to another person today. Be encouraging. Be kind. Be loving. When you do, your words will be like "a honeycomb, sweet to the soul and healing to the bones" (Proverbs 16:24).

Sweet God, please help me speak gracious words to others. Forgive me when I don't and help me to be more like You. In Jesus' name, Amen.

FAITH TO-GO

Visit a beekeeper and learn more about honey and bees. Tell the beekeeper about what Proverbs 16:24 says in the Bible.

51

DANIEL EATS VEGETABLES

DANIEL I

How many of you like to eat vegetables?

Maybe at the sound of the word "vegetables", your nose wrinkles, you shake your head, or you make a funny face in disgust, because you don't like vegetables at all!

Daniel was a holy man. He loved God with all his heart, and he sought to follow Him in every way possible. Daniel lived during a time when his people, the Israelites, were exiled in Babylon. He was chosen by Babylon's ruler, King Nebuchadnezzar, to live in the palace and learn the language and literature (or written stories) of the Babylonians. He and a few other men would be in training for three years, and after that, they would serve King Nebuchadnezzar.

> ## GOD'S DAILY SPECIAL
>
> "Please test your servants for ten days: Give us nothing but vegetables to eat and water to drink."
> Daniel 1:12

The men who were chosen were required to eat the food and drink provided by the king. This created a problem for Daniel and three of his friends (known to us as Shadrach, Meshach, and Abednego). They didn't believe God wanted them to eat the royal food and drink, because it wouldn't be healthy or good for their bodies to eat this way.

So they asked the king's servant to run a test. For ten days, these four friends would eat only vegetables and drink only water. After that, they would be compared to the men who were eating the royal diet. This test would show what foods were better for them.

After ten days, who do you think looked healthier?

Daniel and his friends!

Because of this, the guard gave all the men vegetables and water and took away all of the yummy (and probably unhealthy) royal food and drink. From this point forward, all the men who were training to be the king's servants were very well nourished.

What does this story teach us about food? Vegetables are good for us! They help us grow and help our bodies feel good! There are so many different types of vegetables, too. Find a few you love and eat them on a regular basis. And drink water, too! It is much better for you than drinking sugary sodas.

When you eat, choose wisely like Daniel and his friends. It's easy to eat something quick and simple, but sometimes those aren't the best choices for you. Talk to your mom and dad about what food choices are wise for you.

Dear God, I want to thank You for the story of Daniel. Help me to make wise food choices like he did and to eat healthier foods. Amen.

FAITH TO-GO

Make a point
to eat more
vegetables and
drink more water
this week!

52

WILD LOCUSTS AND HONEY

MATTHEW 3:1-6

Have you ever eaten a wild locust before?

I'm pretty sure most of you have not. I haven't, and I don't think I want to, either. Gross!

Eating a bug does not sound delicious to me. One man in the Bible selected locusts as his food of choice. He ate them while living in the wilderness. I am positive that would not have been my food of choice!

John the Baptist was born to Zechariah and Elizabeth (she was the cousin of Mary, who was Jesus's mom). When John the Baptist was born, his parents knew the Lord had special plans for him. His job was to prepare the way of the Lord. But until it was time to do that, he lived in the wilderness. While living in the wilderness, the Bible says he "grew and became strong in spirit" (Luke 1:80).

> ### GOD'S DAILY SPECIAL
>
> "John's clothes were made of camel's hair, and he had a leather belt around his waist. His food was locusts and wild honey."
> Matthew 3:4

If you lived in the wilderness, what do you think life would be like? You wouldn't be able to go out to eat in restaurants. You wouldn't be able to go shopping for nice clothes to wear. You wouldn't be able to sit on your couch and watch television. You wouldn't have a regular bathroom to use. You wouldn't have access to a hair salon to get a haircut. You wouldn't be able to sleep in a normal bed. And you wouldn't have a regular house to use for shelter. Life would look really different in the wilderness!

None of those things really mattered to John the Baptist, though. The Bible tells us John wore clothes made from camel's hair and wore a leather belt around his waist (Matthew 3:4). He might not have won a fashion award for his wardrobe, but he was comfortable! It also says he ate wild locusts and honey. Oh my! That's probably not what I would have chosen to eat, but I believe God provided those locusts to keep him well-fed, healthy, and ready to do his job.

And John the Baptist was definitely ready! When it was time, he left the wilderness and started preaching about the Messiah (Jesus) who was coming. He told everyone that Jesus would be the Savior of the world. He cried out about the forgiveness of sins through Jesus Christ. Thank you, John, for answering the call of God and preparing the way of the Lord.

Most Holy God, thank You for providing for John the Baptist while in the wilderness. And thank You for using him to tell others about Jesus. Help me to tell others about Jesus, too. Amen.

FAITH TO-GO

Try a new food tonight at dinner, something you have never eaten before. And even if you don't like it, thank God for it.

53

JESUS IS TEMPTED IN THE WILDERNESS

MATTHEW 4:1-11

Has anyone ever tempted you with food? It may have been hard to resist, especially if you were really hungry!

My grandmother used to tell me a story about temptation from her childhood. One day, when she and her sister were kids, they went to the ice cream store. They both got their cones and headed back home. My grandmother was so hungry that she ate her ice cream cone really fast! Her sister, however, was still eating her ice cream when they got home, so she tempted my grandmother with her cone, waving it in her face, saying, "Don't you wish you had some?" My grandmother didn't like that at all, so she slapped the ice cream cone out of her sister's hand. It splattered all over the floor! I think they both got in trouble that day, but my grandmother always told me she wished she hadn't let temptation and jealousy get the best of her. She knew it was wrong.

> ### GOD'S DAILY SPECIAL
>
> "After fasting forty days and forty nights, he was hungry."
> Matthew 4:2

In our story today, Jesus is really hungry. You see, He's been fasting (going without food) in the wilderness for forty days and forty nights. The devil decided he wanted to mess with Jesus and try to tempt Him into doing things He would not normally do. Do you think any of his temptations worked on Jesus?

Of course not!

First, because Jesus was so hungry, the devil tried to tempt Him by telling Him to turn stones into bread. Next, the devil tried to tempt Jesus to throw Himself off a cliff, saying that the angels would save

Him because He was the Son of God. Finally, the devil said Jesus could have all the kingdoms of the world if Jesus would bow down to him.

None of those temptations worked. I love how Jesus responded to each one—He came back with a quote from Scripture. When He spoke the Word of God over each temptation, He had the power of God to resist any temptation from the devil.

That's how you and I can overcome temptation, too! Next time you are tempted to eat something you know you shouldn't eat, say something you know you shouldn't say, or do something you know you shouldn't do, quote a Bible verse and ask God to help you overcome temptation. When we speak God's Word over temptation, we can resist it!

Holy God, help me to resist any temptation that I know is not right. Help me to remember Your Word and use it to help me do what is right. Amen.

FAITH TO-GO

Make a list of things that tempt you. Then pray over each one and write out a Bible verse that can help you.

54

JESUS CALLS THE DISCIPLES

LUKE 5:1-11

How do you get food to eat?

From a grocery store, restaurant, farm, or garden, right? But how does that food make it to your home?

Your parents! They go to the store and buy the food you need to eat. They buy that food with money they make at their jobs. They work hard so they can provide food for your family.

> ### GOD'S DAILY SPECIAL
>
> "When they had done so, they caught such a large number of fish that their nets began to break."
> Luke 5:6

Peter, James, and John had a job. This job also provided food for many other people to eat. Can you guess what that job was?

They were fishermen!

Peter, James, and John had a fishing business. They went out onto the Sea of Galilee in their boats and fished so others could have fish to eat, too. But they didn't fish using fishing poles like we do. They fished using large nets. They would throw the net off the side of the boat, then pull it in when it was full of fish.

On this particular day, they had been fishing for hours and had not caught one single fish. It was not a good day for business! Jesus was preaching on this day, too, but the crowd was pressing in on Him so tightly that He needed some space. He got in the fishing boat and asked Peter, James, and John to go out further from the shore so He could speak to the crowd.

When He had finished speaking, He told Peter to put his nets out into the water. I can just imagine Peter's facial expression. He might have wanted to say, "Already did that. It didn't work." Although they had caught nothing all day, Peter went on to say, "But because you say so, I will let down the nets" (Luke 5:5).

Guess what happened? Their nets were so full of fish that they started breaking! What a miracle!

Because of this miracle, Peter, James, and John left their fishing business and followed Jesus. They spent the next three years learning from Jesus and trusting in Him. And after Jesus left the earth, these men still provided food for people—but this time, they offered spiritual food.

Almighty God, thank You for my parents who work so hard so we can have food to eat. Help me to trust in You for all things. In Jesus' name, Amen.

FAITH TO-GO

Go fishing today! As you fish, remember this story of how Jesus called the disciples to follow Him.

55

JESUS CHANGES WATER INTO WINE

JOHN 2:1-12

Have you ever been to a wedding?

First, you attend the ceremony (which may be a little boring to you), but then, you head to the reception. This is probably the part you have been waiting for because guess what's there? Food, and lots of it!

Receptions are my favorite part of weddings because the food is so yummy, and the cake is delicious! You may be served water or sweet tea to drink (if you live in the South), and your parents and other adults may have the option to drink some wine.

> ## GOD'S DAILY SPECIAL
>
> "What Jesus did here in Cana of Galilee was the first of the signs through which he revealed his glory; and his disciples believed in him."
> John 2:11

Did you know Jesus went to a wedding? He and his mother, Mary, attended a wedding with some of the disciples in the city of Cana. It was probably the wedding of a close family friend or someone Jesus and His mother knew well.

At weddings in Bible times, wine was always served. It was customary for the best wine to be served first. The bride and groom wanted their guests to get the best food and wine at their wedding reception.

Something happened at this wedding that I have never seen happen at a wedding before. They ran out of wine! Not a good moment for the bride and groom (but luckily, I don't think they ever knew they ran out)!

Jesus's mother told Him to help, but Jesus said, "My hour has not yet come" (John 2:4). What Jesus meant was that it wasn't quite time for everyone to know who He was. But it *was* the right time for His disciples and a few others at the wedding to know who Jesus was and what He could do.

Jesus asked the servants to fill six stone jars with water until they were completely full. (These jars could hold between 20-30 gallons of water each, which is a lot of water!) Then, the master of the banquet took a drink from one of the jars and was surprised! He couldn't believe they had saved the best wine for last! But the ones who were really in shock were the servants who filled the jars and Jesus's disciples. Water went into those jars, but wine came out. What a miracle! That was the first miracle Jesus performed. It was done so that His disciples would believe in Him, and they did. I pray that you believe in Jesus, too.

Loving God, thank You for miracles. Help me to believe in You at all times. In Jesus' name, Amen.

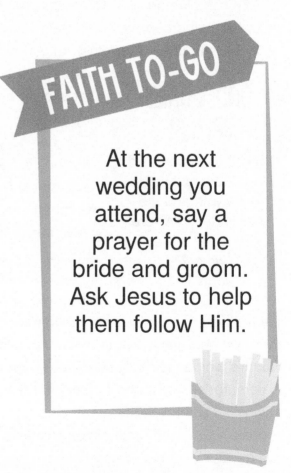

FAITH TO-GO

At the next wedding you attend, say a prayer for the bride and groom. Ask Jesus to help them follow Him.

56

LIVING WATER

JOHN 4:1-42

Do you remember which beverage I love to drink all the time? Water!

Yes, I only drink water. I used to drink lemonade (especially Chick-Fil-A's lemonade), Coca-Cola, and grape Kool-Aid. But one year, I gave up soda for Lent, and I never went back. That eventually led me to give up other sugary drinks, too. I just really love water! It always quenches my thirst, and it especially hits the spot on hot summer days.

In our story today, Jesus is traveling. He stops in Samaria on a really hot day, and I can only imagine He's very thirsty. A woman comes to the well to get some water, so He asks her for a drink. She is shocked for a couple of reasons. First, she's a Samaritan and He's a Jew (and those two groups of people didn't like each other). Secondly, she's a woman and He's a man (and back then, women didn't talk to men in public, except their husbands). So, this woman is really surprised when Jesus asks her for a drink – so surprised that she questions Him about it. Jesus replies by saying, "If you knew the gift of God and who it is that asks you for a drink, you would have asked him and he would have given you living water" (John 4:10).

GOD'S DAILY SPECIAL

"'Sir,' the woman said, 'you have nothing to draw with and the well is deep. Where can you get this living water?'"
John 4:11

What would your reaction have been if Jesus offered to give you living water? I am sure you would have questioned Him, just like she did.

In John 6:27, Jesus said we should work for food that endures, but He wasn't talking about actual food. He was talking about believing in Him so we could live forever with Him one day in heaven. This living water Jesus speaks of isn't real liquid, but it's what allows us to live forever with Him. When we accept Jesus as our Savior, we are given living water. We drink from that water daily by spending time with Jesus: reading our Bible, going to church, worshiping God, and praying. Then we share that living water! So today, go out and share with someone else what Jesus has done for you!

Heavenly Father, thank You for the water I can drink on this earth, but most importantly, thank You for the living water You give me when I accept Jesus as my Savior. Help others to thirst for this same living water and come to know You, too. Amen.

FAITH TO-GO

Pass out bottles of water at a public park and tell others about Jesus.

FOOD TRUCK WORKERS

Running a food truck is not something you can do by yourself. You need help!

In the space below, write down names of people who you would like to work in your food truck. Also write down what jobs you would give them...who would take orders, who would clean, who would drive the truck, who would wash dishes?

FOOD TRUCK
WORKERS

USE THE SPACE BELOW TO DRAW PICTURES OF YOUR FOOD TRUCK
WORKERS. GIVE THEM A COOL UNIFORM TO WEAR!

57

FASTING

MATTHEW 6:16-18

Does your church celebrate the season of Lent?

This church season occurs forty days before Easter, not counting Sundays. It's a time of asking God for forgiveness, fasting, and preparing to celebrate our Risen Lord on Easter Sunday. During Lent, many people give something up for those forty days. People choose all kinds of things to give up, from a type of food to social media, from video games to saying unkind things, from being negative to shopping online. Giving something up is a type of fasting because you are going without that thing for a certain amount of time.

Lent is a great time for you to sacrifice something you love and replace it with reading your Bible, praying, and spending time with Jesus. Fasting during the season of Lent is a wonderful way to grow in your faith.

Did you know the Bible tells us how to fast?

In Matthew 6:16-18, Jesus is teaching a crowd of people about many different things, including fasting. Apparently, back then, there were people who made sure everyone knew when they fasted. They wanted everyone to know they were going without food in order to be closer to God.

> ## GOD'S DAILY SPECIAL
>
> "But when you fast, put oil on your head and wash your face, so that it will not be obvious to others that you are fasting, but only to your Father, who is unseen; and your Father, who sees what is done in secret, will reward you."
> Matthew 6:17-18

Jesus says we should not do that. He doesn't want us to make a big deal about fasting or announce our fasts to the whole world. He doesn't want us to wear a sign that says, "I'm fasting from chocolate." He doesn't need us to draw attention to ourselves and show off what we are doing.

What does God want us to do, then? He wants our fasting to be done in secret, just between us and Him. That doesn't mean you can't tell your parents or someone else close to you what you are fasting from. It's good to have someone to hold you accountable so you don't give in to temptation. Jesus doesn't need us to keep fasting a secret from those who can help us, but He also knows that making a big deal about it misses the point.

So when Lent comes around again (or you decide to fast at another time), don't shout from the rooftops that you are fasting from playing video games. Just chill. Keep it between you and Jesus. And enjoy that time you spend with Him.

Most Awesome God, I want to be closer to You. When I do fast, help me to keep it quiet so that I can focus on You. In Jesus' name, Amen.

FAITH TO-GO

Write down several possible things you would like to fast from for Lent. And then pray about it. Ask God what He would like for you to give up.

58

DO NOT WORRY

MATTHEW 6:25-27

Can I share something with you?

I am a worrier. I don't like to admit it, but I do struggle with worry.

Last year, I had surgery to remove my gallbladder. After the surgery, I thought I'd be able to go back to the foods I had been eating before I had trouble with my gallbladder, but I quickly found out that was not the case. Some foods still caused my stomach to hurt. Honestly, I was worried at first, because I didn't know what I would be able to eat.

God led me to Matthew 6, which reminds us not to worry, and more specifically, not to worry about what we will eat.

"Therefore I tell you, do not worry about your life, what you will eat or drink; or about your body, what you will wear. Is not life more than food, and the body more than clothes?" (Matthew 6:25).

There it was, right there in my Bible: don't worry about what you're going to eat. It felt like God wrote that message just for me. And God did provide food for me to eat. Foods I have never liked or even considered trying are now foods I love. Even better, I feel healthier when I eat these foods! I worried about something God was definitely not worried about. I'm grateful to God for providing food for me to eat that does not hurt my stomach.

> ## GOD'S DAILY SPECIAL
>
> "Therefore I tell you, do not worry about your life, what you will eat or drink; or about your body, what you will wear. Is not life more than food, and the body more than clothes?"
> Matthew 6:25

Do you struggle with worry when it comes to eating food? Maybe you have food allergies, and you worry about accidentally eating something you are allergic to. Maybe a food you love and have eaten for a long time now makes your stomach hurt and you're worried about what you can eat. Or maybe you worry about not having enough food in your house to eat.

I'm here to remind you that God says, "Do not worry." I know it's a struggle because fear can take over our minds really quickly. Sometimes, we just don't know how to stop worrying about food. But we can trust that He will provide the right food for us. And He will keep us safe. May this promise from God bring you peace.

Dear God, please forgive me for worrying about food. Help me to trust in You and believe You will provide food I can eat. Amen.

FAITH TO-GO

If you're worried about food, write down what foods you are worried about. Ask God to take away your worry and give you peace. Then write the words "Do Not Worry" across all the food worry words, because you know God will give you His peace.

59

JESUS EATS WITH SINNERS

LUKE 5:27-36

That's not fair. That isn't right. I can't believe it.

Have you ever muttered those words before?

In the Bible, there was a group of religious people called the Pharisees. They were the rule followers. They did everything according to what the Book of the Law said (which were the rules God gave Moses and the Israelites when they were wandering in the wilderness). But when Jesus came, He brought a new covenant. He said all people could be saved if they believed in Him and asked for forgiveness of their sins. They didn't have to follow those thousands of rules to be in good standing with God anymore.

But the Pharisees had a really hard time believing the things Jesus said. They just didn't like Him.

One day, Jesus called a man named Levi (also known as Matthew) to follow Him as one of His twelve disciples. Levi was a tax collector, and tax collectors were not very well liked, because they usually collected more tax than was needed and kept that money for themselves. They were thieves!

On the same day Jesus called Levi to be His disciple, Levi decided to honor Jesus with a large banquet that included lots of food! When you have a lot of food, you invite a lot of people over. Who do you think Levi invited? He chose all the people he knew well—other tax collectors!

GOD'S DAILY SPECIAL

"Then Levi held a great banquet for Jesus at his house, and a large crowd of tax collectors and others were eating with them."
Luke 5:29

When the Pharisees saw Jesus eating at Levi's house, they went crazy! They could not believe Jesus was eating with a bunch of sinners. They might have thought, "That's not fair! That's not right! I can't believe it!"

I love Jesus's response to the Pharisees' question about why He was eating with tax collectors. He said, "It is not the healthy who need a doctor, but the sick. I have not come to call the righteous, but sinners to repentance" (Luke 5:31-32). Jesus came to the earth so that *all* people could be saved. He loves everyone and wants all of us to live forever with Him one day in heaven. Jesus made a way for everyone to turn from their sinful ways and follow Him.

We are all sinners—every single one of us. I pray you will live your life in a way that points others to Jesus and His forgiveness.

Heavenly Father, forgive me for things I do that are wrong. Help me to live my life by showing others Your light. Amen.

FAITH TO-GO

Has someone you know recently given their life to Jesus? Throw them a party! Celebrate their salvation!

60

THE DISCIPLES PICK GRAIN ON THE SABBATH

MATTHEW 12:1-14

What do you do when you get hungry?

You eat, right? Usually, our stomachs growl when it's time for a meal. We might tell our parents we are hungry so they can satisfy our hunger pains with a delicious meal. Sometimes, they offer us a small snack if it's not time for a meal.

GOD'S DAILY SPECIAL

"At that time Jesus went through the grainfields on the Sabbath. His disciples were hungry and began to pick some heads of grain and eat them."

Matthew 12:1

In our story today, the disciples were hungry, and they just happened to be walking through a grainfield. They picked some of the heads of grain and ate them. I bet their stomachs stopped growling and they were satisfied.

Here's the problem: it was the Sabbath day (the day of rest and no work). Picking grain was considered work. And guess who saw them pick those heads of grain? The Pharisees! They were not happy that the disciples had done this.

They began hammering Jesus with questions, saying that picking grain was unlawful on the Sabbath. How could Jesus let His followers do something that was not right? The Sabbath day was set aside for rest, not work.

Jesus had a great answer. He reminded them about the time David and his companions ate the consecrated bread from the temple (1 Samuel 21:1-9). They were starving that day, and the only food they could find was holy bread that only the priests could eat. But God allowed it because He did not want anyone to go hungry.

At the end of His answer, Jesus says, "Therefore it is lawful to do good on the Sabbath" (Matthew 12:12). Jesus came to set us free from the Law. He came to say that it's okay to do good things on the Sabbath—things like picking grain from the field so you won't go hungry, saving your sheep from a pit so they won't die, or healing the sick. All of these things are work, but they are good work, so they are fine to do on the Sabbath.

Does Jesus want us to rest? Yes, absolutely. But He doesn't want us to go hungry, refuse to help a friend, or stop saving our animals on the Sabbath. He wants us to do those things because they are good.

Loving God, thank You for providing food for us to eat. Help me learn to share my food with others so they will not go hungry. Amen.

FAITH TO-GO

After church on a Sunday, go out together as a family and do something good and kind for others.

61

FRUITS OF THE TREE

LUKE 6:43-45

What do you expect to find growing on an apple tree? Apples, of course!

What do you expect to find growing on an orange tree? Oranges, of course!

You'll never come across an apple tree that is growing oranges or an orange tree that is growing apples. It just doesn't happen.

In our story today, we find Jesus using the example of a tree and its fruit to describe the character of a person. The tree stands for our hearts, and the fruit stands for our actions and our words.

Jesus says, "A good man brings good things out of the good stored up in his heart, and an evil man brings evil things out of the evil stored up in his heart. For the mouth speaks what the heart is full of" (Luke 6:45).

> ## GOD'S DAILY SPECIAL
>
> "No good tree bears bad fruit, nor does a bad tree bear good fruit. Each tree is recognized by its own fruit."
> Luke 6:43-44

Basically, Jesus is saying that whatever is in your heart will overflow out of your mouth and into your actions. If what's in your heart is good, what you do and say will be good. If what's in your heart is bad, what you do and say will be bad.

I love when Jesus points out, "Each tree is recognized by its own fruit" (Luke 6:44). Just like an apple tree is known for growing apples, a person will be recognized by what they do and what they say.

What kind of person do you want others to see when they look at your life? I don't know about you, but I want others to see the good in me. I want them to see how much I love Jesus through the way I treat the people around me.

Will you and I mess up? Yes, of course! But we know Jesus forgives us when we ask. We know this because we know Jesus. We believe He died for our sins (all the bad things we do) so we can live forever with Him one day in heaven. I am so very grateful for that!

What kind of tree are you? Think about it, and if you need to change your heart or seek forgiveness, ask God, who graciously forgives us of all our sins!

Thank You, God, for forgiving me when I mess up. Help my heart to always pour forth good words and good actions. Help me to be a tree that bears good fruit. Amen.

FAITH TO-GO

Bake a pie with your favorite fruit.
Deliver it to your neighbor.

62

FEEDING OF THE 5,000

JOHN 6:1-15

The miracle in our Bible reading today is very popular. You have probably heard this story before, at church or from your own Bible reading time. If so, you remember that Jesus took five small barley loaves and two small fish, blessed them, and used them to feed 5,000 men plus even more women and children. That would have been an amazing miracle to witness!

I like to read the Bible and see it through the eyes of the characters in each story. If I were one of the people in this story, what would I have done? What would I have said?

Let's look at this story through the eyes of the young boy who had the loaves and fish with him...

> ## GOD'S DAILY SPECIAL
>
> "Here is a boy with five small barley loaves and two small fish, but how far will they go among so many?"
> John 6:9

He was hungry, and he was so glad his mom had packed his lunch. He had heard Jesus was going to the town of Bethsaida, and he wanted to hear Him teach. Jesus was famous because He could heal people and perform miracles. His family couldn't wait to listen to the wise teachings of Jesus.

His stomach began to rumble. It had been a long day, and he thought everyone else was probably as hungry as he was, too. He opened his family's basket and found five small barley loaves and two small fish to eat. As his family began unpacking their food, Andrew, one of Jesus's disciples, came by to ask if anyone had food. He raised his hand and shouted to Andrew that he did! Andrew quickly asked him to come—and to bring the food with him. He looked at his parents, who told him to go. If a disciple of Jesus asks you to go, you go, of course!

Andrew showed Jesus the boy's food. It wasn't much - just five small loaves and two small fish. What could Jesus do with this? Did He want it for Himself?

Jesus did the opposite of what everyone expected. He blessed the boy's bread and fish and it multiplied! Suddenly, there was enough bread and fish for more than 5,000 people to eat! How could this be? Just a minute ago, it was only enough for the boy and his family. Now it was enough for the huge crowd of people! They even took up twelve baskets of leftovers! The boy could not believe it. He had witnessed a miracle, and he thought it was so cool that Jesus had used his food to feed everyone!

What an amazing experience! Jesus used what the boy had and turned it into enough for everyone. I'm sure that young boy talked about this miracle for many years.

Miracles still happen today. Do you see them? Just open your eyes and ears to see and listen to the everyday miracles Jesus is still performing today.

Heavenly Father, thank You for using such a small amount of food to feed so many people. Help me to see the small miracles You give me every day. Amen.

FAITH TO-GO

Make a list of big or small miracles Jesus has done for you or your family. Say a prayer thanking God for these miracles.

63

WORKING FOR FOOD THAT ENDURES FOREVER

JOHN 6:25-29

When I was in high school, I had a job at one of my favorite places, Chick-Fil-A! I mostly worked as a cashier, but sometimes I cooked the food, and other times I washed the dishes. I think I actually liked cooking food the most!

GOD'S DAILY SPECIAL

"Do not work for food that spoils, but for food that endures to eternal life, which the Son of Man will give you."
John 6:27

I worked for 4-6 hours at a time after school or on the weekends (I especially loved that I got Sundays off). I loved working hard, but I also couldn't wait to take a break to eat some of their tasty food. I still really love Chick-Fil-A!

In our Bible story today, a crowd of people have been following Jesus around, listening to His teachings. They've loved learning from Him so much that they jump on boats and travel around to find Him when He moves on to the next town.

One day, a crowd finally found Jesus on the other side of a lake. When they asked how long He had been there, He responded by saying they only followed Him there because He fed them bread (He was referencing the story we just read yesterday). He then goes on to tell them that they should not "work for food that spoils, but for food that endures to eternal life" (John 6:27).

They must have been scratching their heads on that one. What kind of food must they work for that endures to eternal life (which means lives forever)?

Jesus answers...

"The work of God is this: to believe in the one he has sent" (John 6:29).

Believing in Jesus as our Savior is the food that lasts forever. This means we should seek Him daily by spending time with Him, seek forgiveness for our sins on a daily basis, and share our belief in Jesus so others can believe and live forever with Him, too.

Go out today and work for spiritual food that lasts forever. Believe in Jesus and go tell others about Him!

Loving God, thank You for sending Jesus to be our Savior. Help me work hard every day at being a faithful follower of You. In Jesus' name, Amen.

FAITH TO-GO

Go through the drive-through at Chick-Fil-A today. Do a random act of kindness and pay for the meal of the person behind you.

FOOD TRUCK FIRST STOP

Oh the places you can go with a food truck! So many different types of places you can park your truck and serve up some yummy food!

In the space below, write down some places you would like to go with your food truck. Which of these places would you like to stop at first?

FOOD TRUCK FIRST STOP

DRAW A PICTURE OF YOUR FOOD TRUCK AT ITS FIRST STOP.
DRAW YOUR TRUCK, AS WELL AS PEOPLE LINED UP TO GET YOUR FOOD!

64

BREAD OF LIFE

JOHN 6:30-40

Recently, my daughter asked me to get something for her at the grocery store. She usually requests candy, cookies, or ice cream, but this time she only wanted one thing: sub sandwich rolls. You know, the round, yummy bread you can find at any sub sandwich shop. She wanted to start making sandwiches for school with this type of bread.

I bought it for her, and she was excited to make that first sandwich! She couldn't wait to eat sub sandwiches for at least five more days—an entire week of school lunches!

But something had happened when she got ready to make another sandwich the next day. The bread had started molding. Blue and white patches were already forming all over each sub roll. It smelled bad and it was gross! The bread didn't last long enough for her to enjoy, and she was so upset.

Unlike sub sandwich rolls, there is a Bread that will last forever. That Bread is Jesus.

> ## GOD'S DAILY SPECIAL
>
> "Then Jesus declared, 'I am the bread of life. Whoever comes to me will never go hungry, and whoever believes in me will never be thirsty.'"
> John 6:35

In our verses today, Jesus calls Himself the Bread of Life. This doesn't mean that Jesus is actually a piece of bread. The bread is a symbol of Jesus Himself. These verses explain that if we believe in Him, we will never be spiritually hungry or thirsty again. We will still be hungry and thirsty for physical food and drink, but Jesus, the Bread of Life, will fill us up spiritually forever.

Jesus says one more thing, and it's the most important thing for us to hear. In John 6:40, Jesus says, "For my Father's will is that everyone who looks to the Son and believes in him shall have eternal life."

Did you catch that? If we believe in Jesus, we can live forever with Him in heaven one day. Accepting Jesus as your Savior is THE most important decision you will ever make in your life. It's a decision about your eternity. God wants all His children to accept Jesus as their Savior, believe that He died on the cross for our sins, and trust in His love for us. I want you to believe, too. If you haven't already accepted Jesus as your Savior, you can pray right now, asking God to forgive you for the wrong things you have done and telling Him you believe in Jesus and accept Him as your Savior.

Jesus is your Bread of Life. Accept this Bread and you will live forever in heaven with Him one day.

Loving God, thank You for sending Jesus to die on the cross for me. Help me to follow Him all the days of my life. I love You, Lord. Amen.

FAITH TO-GO

If you have been saved by Jesus (meaning you have accepted Him as your Savior), tell someone! Let others know that Jesus is your Savior.

65

THE GREAT BANQUET

LUKE 14:15-24

At every great banquet or party, you'll find lots of food. You might see some of your favorite foods: chicken nuggets, macaroni and cheese, french fries, pizza, lasagna, tacos, burritos, nachos, hamburgers, corn on the cob, and mashed potatoes. And don't forget the desserts: chocolate chip cookies, brownies, ice cream, apple pie, and chocolate cake. Is your mouth watering yet?

If you were invited to a big banquet or party, would you turn that invitation down? Probably not, right? But lots of people did that in our story today. Why would they do such a thing?

GOD'S DAILY SPECIAL

"Jesus replied: 'A certain man was preparing a great banquet and invited many guests."
Luke 14:16

In today's Bible reading, Jesus tells a parable (a story) about a man who prepared a banquet for the people in his town. He sent out invitations and got busy preparing for his party. When it was ready, he sent his servant out to bring the guests in. But there was a problem. The guests started making excuses about why they couldn't attend. One bought a field and had to go see it. One just bought five oxen and wanted to put them to work right away. Another said he had just gotten married. Were these good excuses? Not really.

This made the host of the banquet upset! He told his servant to go into the streets and invite the poor, the blind, the lame, and the crippled. So he did, and they came, but there was *still* more room.

The servant went out again and invited even more people until the banquet was full.

The parables of Jesus always have a meaning. In this parable, the host of the banquet is Jesus. He has prepared a place for us to live with Him one day in heaven. We will eat at His heavenly banquet. We can go to this eternal party because He has invited us.

But some people turn this gift down. They make excuses about why they don't want to know Jesus or accept His gift of salvation. That makes Jesus sad, and it makes me sad, too. But I can keep praying for them. That's what you can do, too. Together, let's pray all of God's children will accept His invitation to the Great Banquet and will come to know Jesus as their Savior.

Loving God, show me who needs to know You. Help me to pray daily for their salvation. And help me to be a good friend and share Your love with them. Amen.

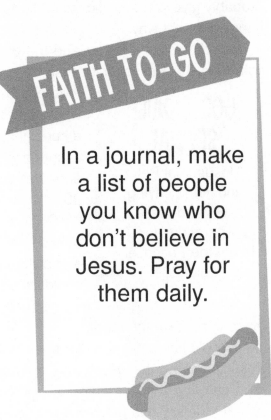

FAITH TO-GO

In a journal, make a list of people you know who don't believe in Jesus. Pray for them daily.

66

PREPARE FOR THE MEAL

LUKE 22:7-13

Have you ever helped your parents prepare dinner? Maybe you helped by setting the table, tossing the salad, cutting up the vegetables, or making the dessert. When you help your parents, they probably give you specific instructions or even show you how to do things the right way.

In today's story, Jesus and the disciples were in Jerusalem to celebrate the Passover (a festival that Jewish people celebrated to remember the night God saved them when they were slaves in Egypt). It was a special meal with specific instructions according to what God had told Moses all those years ago (see Exodus 12:1-28).

> ### GOD'S DAILY SPECIAL
>
> "Jesus sent Peter and John, saying, 'Go and make preparations for us to eat the Passover.'"
> Luke 22:8

On the night of the Passover, Jesus asked Peter and John to go into the city and prepare the Passover meal so they could all eat together. But Jesus didn't just say, "go," He gave them instructions, including how to find a place to prepare the meal.

Jesus's instructions might seem a little strange to you. He told Peter and John that when they entered the city, they would see a man carrying a jar of water. When they met him, they were supposed to follow this man to a house and enter it with him. Now, if I were Peter and John, I might have asked Jesus a few questions before I went to prepare the Passover:

How will we know which man is the right one? How do we know he will lead us to the right place? Are you sure about this, Jesus?

Maybe they didn't ask questions, though, because they knew Jesus and trusted Him not to lead them astray. But here's the cool thing: in Bible times, men did not carry jars of water around. That was usually a job for women. So the disciples knew that if they saw a man carrying water, he'd be the one the Lord sent.

When they got into town, they did find a man carrying a jar of water! He led them to a house, and in that house was a furnished upper room. They prepared to eat the Passover meal there with Jesus and the other disciples (which involved preparing a lamb to eat, along with bread and herbs).

What I love most about this story is that the disciples trusted Jesus and obeyed what He said to them, even if it didn't make sense at the time. They did this because they had faith in Him, and their faith moved them to obey. I pray your faith in God will move you to obey what He calls you to do, too.

Father God, help me to follow You at all times. Amen.

FAITH TO-GO

Prepare your own lunch for school. Pack an extra sandwich or snacks to give to someone who needs it.

67

A MEAL TO REMEMBER

LUKE 22:14-23

Do you remember what you had for supper last night? How about what you had for lunch a week ago, or what you ate last year on your birthday?

If you can remember those things, you are doing well! Sadly, I am not so good at this. I can barely remember what I ate earlier today, much less what I ate a week ago or a year ago on my birthday!

Jesus told His disciples (and He tells us, too) to remember Him when we eat. He didn't say this about just any meal, although we should give Him thanks anytime we eat. He tells us to remember Him when we eat bread and drink wine or grape juice. This meal is called communion. It's a special meal, usually eaten at church with other believers in Jesus. Sometimes, we also take communion at camps, on retreats, or on other special occasions.

> ## GOD'S DAILY SPECIAL
>
> "And he took bread, gave thanks and broke it, and gave it to them, saying, 'This is my body given for you; do this in remembrance of me."
> Luke 22:19

The communion tradition began on the night of Jesus's Last Supper with His disciples. Remember yesterday's story? Jesus asked His disciples to prepare the Passover meal for them to eat. During the meal, Jesus took bread, gave thanks, and broke it. As He did, He told His disciples that this was His body, broken for them. Whenever they ate it, they should remember Him. Then, He took the cup (of wine), gave thanks, blessed it, and told them it was His blood, shed for them. Whenever they drank it, they should remember Him.

At the time, I think they probably had no clue what He was talking about. But after His death and resurrection, I believe the disciples knew instantly what His words meant. Jesus wanted all of us to have a special meal—one that helps us to remember Him when we eat it.

Why is it important to remember Jesus during this meal? Because as Christians, sometimes we forget the greatest gift Jesus gave to us: He died on the cross for our sins. He loves us so much that He gave His life for us. On the cross, His body was broken (what the bread symbolizes) and His blood was shed (what the juice/wine symbolizes). We need to remember the great love He has for each of us. He loved us so much that He gave up His life so we could live forever with Him in heaven. That's something I don't want to ever forget!

The next time you take communion, remember Jesus. Don't view it as a snack to eat in church because you're hungry. View it as a time to stop and give thanks to Jesus for His sacrifice for you. As you remember that, ask Him to help you live your life for Him.

Holy God, thank You for this meal of remembrance. Help me to remember Your faithfulness and Your love for me every time I take communion. Amen.

FAITH TO-GO

After you take communion at church, go back to your seat and write down five things you remember about Jesus. And then give thanks to God for Jesus.

68

FISH FOR BREAKFAST

JOHN 21:1-14

My grandfather loved to fish. He wasn't one of those fishermen that just went fishing as a hobby. He caught fish because he loved to eat them! I remember him going fishing when we visited his house, and he always caught a lot of fish. He would put the fish into a cooler and bring them home. Then he would cook them in his fish fryer. They were so good! I always loved having dinner at their house when it was fish fry night!

GOD'S DAILY SPECIAL

"When they landed, they saw a fire of burning coals there with fish on it, and some bread."
John 21:9

We ate fish a lot, but I don't ever remember eating fish for breakfast. Have you ever done that? I do know of some people who ate fish for breakfast. Jesus and His disciples did that one early morning after His resurrection.

Some of the disciples had been out fishing all night and couldn't catch anything. Early the next morning, they saw a man on the shore, but they didn't recognize him. He asked them if they had any fish to eat. When they said no, he told them if they threw their net over the side of the boat, they would catch plenty of fish. And they did. They caught 153 fish, to be exact!

The man who had given them this advice was Jesus. As soon as Peter recognized Him, he jumped off the boat and swam to shore. He was so excited to see Jesus that he couldn't wait to row the boat to shore. He had to jump in and swim instead!

When the other disciples came ashore, Jesus invited them to eat breakfast with Him. He was already cooking some fish and bread over a fire. Breakfast with Jesus was served!

What a memorable meal the disciples must have had with their risen Savior! It was a peaceful morning on the beach. A fire was blazing, cooking fish for everyone. But the most memorable thing about this breakfast wasn't the food. It was the presence of Jesus. He made this a breakfast the disciples would never forget.

Jesus's presence is still with us today. We can't see Him with our eyes, but we know He is there because the Bible tells us He is always with us. I am so grateful for that!

Loving God, thank You for breakfast. Help me to remember You every morning when I get up and have breakfast. Remind me of Your presence throughout the day. Amen.

FAITH TO-GO

Go fishing with your parents, grandparents, or a friend. Take a cooler with you to keep the fish as you catch them. Then take them home for a fish fry!

69

BREAKING BREAD TOGETHER

ACTS 2:42-47

I grew up going to church, and some of my favorite childhood church memories are the times we ate together! My church used to have breakfast once a month before Sunday School. I absolutely loved this, because I got to eat donuts, muffins, breakfast casserole, cinnamon rolls, and fruit. It was awesome!

We also used to have covered dish suppers (people bring food from home to share with everyone at this kind of meal). I loved those, too, because I got to eat food I wasn't normally served at home—especially all those yummy desserts. It was a highlight for me!

> ## GOD'S DAILY SPECIAL
>
> "They devoted themselves to the apostles' teaching and to fellowship, to the breaking of bread and to prayer."
> Acts 2:42

I liked more than just the food at those church meals. I really enjoyed eating with my church friends. I loved sitting down and talking with them over a meal. I loved our conversations, but I mostly enjoyed simply getting to hang out with them.

Our practice of eating together at church comes straight out of the Bible. It's something the very first believers in Jesus did together: "They devoted themselves to...the breaking of bread" (Acts 2:42). Breaking of bread means eating together in this Scripture. When the Bible says "breaking of bread," it refers to a group of people having a meal together.

Here's the backstory to this passage: Jesus rose from the dead and spent forty more days on earth before ascending (going up) to heaven. He told the disciples to wait in Jerusalem until the arrival of the Holy Spirit.

On the day of Pentecost, the Holy Spirit descended on the disciples, and they began preaching and teaching others about Jesus. On this day, more than 3,000 people believed in Jesus as their Savior.

This is where our story picks up.

Today's verses tell us that these new believers spent time listening to the teaching of the apostles (the disciples), hanging out with each other (fellowship), eating together (breaking bread), and praying. They offer us a wonderful example of how to live as Christians.

Great conversations about our faith in God can happen while we eat meals with fellow Christians, especially our families. All distractions are put aside so we can focus on each other.

Whether you're attending a church event that involves food, or it's just another day at home eating dinner with your family, enjoy the fellowship with other believers in Jesus and remember that the early Christians did the same thing.

Awesome God, thank You for the food You give me. Help my family to eat dinner together and spend more time with You. Help us to grow in our faith in You. Amen.

FAITH TO-GO

Ask your parents if you can help cook dinner for your family tonight. Plan out the menu and help your parents cook. Then enjoy dinner together as a family!

70

THE WIDOWS ARE NEGLECTED

ACTS 6:1-7

Have you ever been left out? Maybe you didn't get invited to a friend's birthday party. Maybe your sibling wouldn't share their favorite toy with you. Maybe you didn't get to attend a special event because you got grounded. No matter what, it's not fun being left out.

Did you know that when the church was just beginning, some people felt left out? It's true! I don't think this was intentional, but it did happen!

GOD'S DAILY SPECIAL

"In those days when the number of disciples was increasing, the Hellenistic Jews among them complained against the Hebraic Jews because their widows were being overlooked in the daily distribution of food."
Acts 6:1

At this time in the church, the widows (women whose husbands had died) were left out of the daily distribution of food. Jesus had told His disciples (and He tells us, too) to take care of the widows and the orphans (kids who don't have parents).

Thankfully, some people noticed the widows weren't getting any food and decided to solve the problem. It caused a little bit of conflict, but the disciples took it seriously and came up with a plan.

The disciples selected seven men to be responsible for taking care of the widows in the church. One of the men chosen was named Stephen, a man who later died because of his faith in Jesus. He was known as the first martyr. These seven men were brought before the disciples, who laid their hands on them and prayed over them, blessing them with the Lord's power.

These seven men took care of the widows so the disciples could focus on praying and sharing the Word of God. Guess what happened because of the church's faithfulness to God? The message of Jesus spread like wildfire! Many people came to believe in Jesus because these men faithfully spread the Good News to everyone.

When was the last time you shared Jesus with someone else? If we did this every day, I believe the name of Jesus would spread, and the number of believers would increase rapidly (just like it said it did in Acts 6:7).

What are you waiting for? Be a faithful follower of Jesus and share His love with someone today!

Holy God, I want to be a faithful follower of You, just like the disciples. Show me who needs to hear about You today and help me to be bold and share Your love with them. Amen.

FAITH TO-GO

Do you know a widow in your church or neighborhood? Take them dinner one night and tell them that Jesus loves them!

FOOD TRUCK PRAYER

Everything we do needs to be covered in prayer! Your new food truck ministry needs to be prayed over.

In the space below, write down a few things about your ministry that you need God to help you with, or that you want God to bless.

FOOD TRUCK PRAYER

NOW IT'S TIME TO WRITE OUT YOUR PRAYER. IN THE SPACE BELOW, WRITE OUT A PRAYER TO GOD ASKING HIM TO BLESS YOUR FOOD TRUCK.

71

SAUL'S CONVERSION

ACTS 9:1-19

Saul did not like Christians at all. He was a Pharisee, which means he was a religious Jewish man who followed the Old Testament law. And Jesus, whom everyone loved, was doing things that just did not go along with what Saul believed. This man did miracles, healed people, brought people back from the dead, ate with sinners - all things that just seemed crazy to Saul.

Do you know what Saul did? He persecuted the believers (the new Christians who believed in Jesus). He went from house to house, taking them away and putting them in prison. He even killed some of them. He really did not like the name of Jesus being spread.

But Jesus did something amazing. He turned Saul into a man who loved Jesus with all his heart.

Jesus spoke to Saul on the way to Damascus by sending a bright light and

> ### GOD'S DAILY SPECIAL
>
> "For three days he was blind, and did not eat or drink anything."
> Acts 9:9

saying, "Saul, Saul, why do you persecute me?" (Acts 9:4). Jesus told Saul to go into the city, and once he got there, Jesus would tell him what to do next.

But there was a problem: because of that bright light, Saul could no longer see! His friends who were traveling with him had to guide him into Damascus. I can only imagine how freaked out Saul must have been. First, he saw a bright light and heard the voice of Jesus talking to him. Then he was blinded by the bright light and couldn't see anything. He had to be a little scared!

During this time of blindness, do you think Saul had a party? Do you think he ate a lot of food? He'd just heard the voice of Jesus, so why not celebrate, right?

No, Saul did not do any of that. Actually, he fasted for three days. No big meals, no parties, and no celebrating that he had just heard a message from Jesus. Instead, he spent those three days in prayer. When major moments with Jesus happen to you (like they did to him), the only thing you want to do is pray to God. Back then, a lot of people fasted while they prayed. So, while Saul spent three days without sight, he also went without food. He listened to God and believed the vision he had received (which was that a man named Ananias would heal him).

Guess what? Saul *was* healed! After this, he turned from a man who hated Christians into a man who believed in Jesus so much that he went out and preached His love everywhere he possibly could. That is a miracle in itself!

Most Holy God, thank You for turning Saul's life around. Help me to be like Saul and go out and shout to everyone about Your love. In Jesus' name, Amen.

FAITH TO-GO

Do you know someone who does not believe in Jesus? Write their name down and then commit to praying for them every day.

72

A MEAL AT THE JAILER'S HOUSE

ACTS 16:16-36

I love to have people over for dinner, whether it's for a special occasion (like birthdays or Christmas) or having my daughters' friends over for a meal. I love to cook a meal for my family or my friends, and I love the conversations we have while we eat.

A man in our story today invited some new friends over to dinner at his house. This man was a jailer (a guard at a jail) who invited two surprising guests to his house. He asked Paul (whose name used to be Saul) and Silas over for dinner. You might be asking, "Why is that surprising?" It's shocking because Paul and Silas had just been prisoners in this man's jail! But in this story, we learn that the jailer invited them over because of something they did for him.

Paul and Silas were in prison because they had healed a girl (who was a slave) from evil spirits. Her owners were very upset with Paul and Silas, because they made a lot of money from her fortune-telling. In fact, her owners were so mad that they dragged Paul and Silas into the city, where they faced a judge and were thrown into prison.

> ## GOD'S DAILY SPECIAL
>
> "The jailer brought them into his house and set a meal before them; he was filled with joy because he had come to believe in God – he and his whole household."
> Acts 16:34

But being in prison didn't stop Paul and Silas from praising Jesus or telling others about Him. While in prison, they sang songs to God and prayed. All the other prisoners listened while they did these things.

One night, an earthquake came and freed the chains off every prisoner. When the jailer woke up and discovered what had happened, he was afraid and was about to take his own life (because he knew he would be in so much trouble). But Paul and Silas stopped him! They reassured him that no one ran away—all the prisoners were still there. After this, the jailer asked them how to be saved (I believe he was listening to them sing and pray in prison, too).

On that day, the jailer gave his life to Jesus—and he wanted to celebrate! That's why he brought Paul and Silas to his home and fed them a nice meal. Paul and Silas shared about Jesus with the jailer's family, and they were all saved and baptized that night. What an amazing day for the jailer and his family!

Almighty God, You are awesome! Thank You for helping me learn about the many ways other followers of You share about Your love. Help me to be bold and to share my faith in You through my words and my actions. Amen.

FAITH TO-GO

Invite friends over to your house (ask your parents first). Cook them a meal and then share with them about your love for Jesus.

73

THE SHIPWRECK

ACTS 27:27-44

Paul really trusted God. He believed with all his heart that God was always with him, even on a boat in the middle of a storm.

This storm was fierce. It's definitely not one you or I would want to be in. Can you imagine how much a boat would get tossed around in the sea when heavy winds, rain, and super high waves came along? I think I would get seasick for sure! What about you?

So why was Paul in a boat in the sea in the middle of a storm anyway?

He was a prisoner that was being transferred to the prison in Rome, Italy. 276 passengers were aboard that ship, and I bet they were all terrified of the storm. If I was on that boat, I would have been afraid that it would sink.

While everyone was scared, an angel visited Paul and told him not to be afraid. The angel said every life on that ship would survive! Because of this, everyone onboard continued to believe in the God that Paul trusted.

It was a big deal for these people to trust God, because they had been without food for two whole weeks! They didn't get to eat anything during the storm. Maybe they were so busy trying to stay alive that they forgot to eat. Maybe they decided not to eat because they felt so seasick. Paul says they didn't eat because they were in constant

> ## GOD'S DAILY SPECIAL
>
> "Just before dawn Paul urged them all to eat. 'For the last fourteen days,' he said, 'you have been in constant suspense and have gone without food – you haven't eaten anything.'"
> Acts 27:33

suspense, which means they were probably so worried about what was going to happen to them that they just couldn't eat!

Finally, Paul urged them to eat something. He told them they needed food to survive, and he reminded them that God was with them and had promised Paul that not one of them was going to die on that ship.

Then, Paul did something cool. He took some bread, gave thanks to God, and began eating. This was such an encouragement to the other passengers that they also ate until they were full. Paul encouraged them to eat so they would have the strength to survive. And they did!

Have you ever lost your appetite because you were so worried about something? Next time that happens, take time to pray, asking God to help you let go of that worry. Then, go to the kitchen and fix yourself something to eat. Food does amazing things to help us feel well and also gives us strength. I believe eating will help you feel so much better!

Almighty God, sometimes I worry. And for that I am sorry. Help me to let go of all the worry I hold and to trust in You. In Jesus' name, Amen.

FAITH TO-GO

Do you know a friend who is worried about something? Share some food with them and let them know you are praying for them.

74

EAT AND DRINK FOR GOD'S GLORY

I CORINTHIANS 10:31

Just do it.

I'm sure you've heard that phrase on TV, worn it on a t-shirt, or seen it plastered on a billboard beside the interstate. That's the slogan for Nike, an athletic company that helps you gain confidence in playing sports!

Nike might be popular for this phrase, but I like to say that the Bible coined this term first. In 1 Corinthians 10:31, Paul says, "So whether you eat or drink or whatever you do, do it all for the glory of God." Paul doesn't say the word "just," but I like to insert it and say, "Just do it all for the glory of God."

> ## GOD'S DAILY SPECIAL
> "So whether you eat or drink or whatever you do, do it all for the glory of God."
> 1 Corinthians 10:31

In this passage, Paul is talking to new Christians about their freedom in Christ. He specifically talks about meals and foods they eat. While it can be a little confusing to read because we don't understand their customs or culture, we can see that Paul is telling new believers that everything they do and say (which includes eating and drinking) should be done to glorify God. He also reminds them to do all things for the good of others so we don't cause them to stumble.

Let me give you an example.

Let's say during the season of Lent (remember when we talked about Lent in devotion 57?), your friend has chosen to give up ice cream. They love ice cream. They eat it often because they just can't get enough of it! But they gave it up for Lent because they wanted to spend more time with God instead of eating ice cream.

Usually, when your friend comes over for a sleepover, you make ice cream sundaes. You and your friend have always loved eating ice cream sundaes together. But what should you do in this situation, when your friend has given up ice cream for Lent? Should you still make ice cream sundaes and eat them with your friend? Should you eat your sundae in front of your friend while he or she watches you? Or should you totally skip the ice cream sundaes all together?

In these verses, Paul tells us we should not cause another person to stumble, we should do good to others, and we should eat and drink to glorify God. So the best choice for us in this scenario would be totally skipping the ice cream sundaes at the sleepover. Eating them with our friend would cause them to stumble, and eating them in front of our friend would not bring glory to God.

Go out today and "just do it all for the glory of God." Every action and every word should bring honor to our Lord. And that includes what we eat and what we drink.

Holy God, may my words and my actions always glorify Your name. Help me to choose foods and drinks that bring honor to You. Amen.

FAITH TO-GO

Make a sign that says, "Just do it all for the glory of God." Hang it in your room to remind you of 1 Corinthians 10:31.

75

GENEROUS GIVING

2 CORINTHIANS 9:6-11

Before you open your Bible to read the verses above from 2 Corinthians, I want to share with you the translation of verses 10-11 from The Message. This is my favorite translation of these verses. I think it helps us understand how generous giving relates to food in the Bible.

"This most generous God who gives seed to the farmer that becomes bread for your meals is more than extravagant with you. He gives you something you can then give away, which grows into full-formed lives, robust in God, wealthy in every way, so that you can be generous in every way, producing with us great praise to God" (2 Corinthians 9:10-11).

GOD'S DAILY SPECIAL

"Now he who supplies seed to the sower and bread for food will also supply and increase your store of seed and will enlarge the harvest of your righteousness."
2 Corinthians 9:10

Before this book, had you ever thought about where your food actually comes from? I'm sure most of us don't think about where the food we put into our mouths is actually grown. I love the way Paul (the author of 2 Corinthians) explains that God gives seed to the farmer, which the farmer grows into food for us. God doesn't just give us a little, but He gives us a lot.

What should we do with all the food God provides for us?

Part of the verse tells us exactly what we should do...

"He gives you something you can then give away" (2 Corinthians 9:11).

Maybe you are blessed with a lot of food. You have plenty of food on your table at dinner. You bring enough food to eat for lunch at school. You have a good breakfast every morning, too. If you have more than enough food, God says you should give to others who don't have as much. He gives to us so that we can in turn bless others. When we bless others, it reminds us to be thankful and praise God!

Tonight, when you sit down together at the dinner table, thank God for blessing your family with food. Ask God to show you ways to give some extra food away. God always blesses us so we can be a blessing to others.

Generous God, thank You for blessing me with food to eat. Help me to share that food with others who are in need. Amen.

FAITH TO-GO

Volunteer to help serve food at a local soup kitchen.

FOOD FOR THOUGHT

You did it! You read 75 devotions about food in the Bible, and you created your own food truck ministry! Use this space to write down some things you learned about God.

NEW FOOD STORIES I LEARNED

BIBLE VERSE TO MEMORIZE

HOW GOD SPOKE TO ME

BIBLE STORY TO SHARE

My FOOD TRUCK MINISTRY

NOW IT'S TIME TO PUT ALL YOUR FOOD TRUCK IDEAS TOGETHER. DRAW THE FINAL SET-UP OF YOUR FOOD TRUCK AND HOW IT WILL LOOK!

ABOUT THE AUTHOR

Vanessa Myers has a passion for teaching the Word of God to children and helping them come to know Jesus. She loves to help families live out their faith by equipping them with fun, simple resources to use at home.

Vanessa serves as a Children's Ministry Director in the local church and also enjoys writing books for kids, as well as blogging about all things related to Children's Ministry. You can find these resources on her website: www.vanessamyers.org. She is married to Andrew and they have two daughters.

Made in the USA
Monee, IL
13 April 2022

94636693R00111